ETHICS THROUGH LITERATURE

THE MENAHAM STERN JERUSALEM LECTURES

Sponsored by the Historical Society of Israel
and published for Brandeis University by
University Press of New England

SERIES EDITORS
Yosef Kaplan, Senior Editor, Department of the History of the Jewish People, The Hebrew University of Jerusalem, former chairman of the Historical Society of Israel
Michael Heyd, Department of History, The Hebrew University of Jerusalem, former chairman of the Historical Society of Israel
Shulamit Shahar, professor emeritus, Department of History, Tel-Aviv University, member of the Board of Directors of the Historical Society of Israel

For a complete list of books in this series, please visit www.upne.com and www.upne.com/series/MSL.html

ETHICS through LITERATURE

LITERATURE

Ascetic and Aesthetic Reading
in Western Culture

Brian Stock

THE MENAHEM STERN JERUSALEM LECTURES

Brandeis
University
Press

Historical
Society of
Israel

PUBLISHED BY UNIVERSITY PRESS OF NEW ENGLAND
Hanover and London

Brandeis University Press / Historical Society of Israel
Published by University Press of New England,
One Court Street, Lebanon, NH 03766
www.upne.com

Library of Congress Cataloging-in-Publication Data

Stock, Brian.
Ethics through literature : ascetic and aesthetic reading
in Western culture / Brian Stock.
    p.   cm. — (The Menaham Stern Jerusalem lectures)
Includes bibliographical references and index.
ISBN-13: 978–1–58465–699–9 (cloth : alk. paper)
ISBN-10: 1–58465–699–9 (cloth : alk. paper)
1. Literature and morals. I. Title.
PN49.S824   2007
809'.93353 — dc22   2007044805

green
press
INITIATIVE

University Press of New England is a member of the
Green Press Initiative. The paper used in this book
meets their minimum requirement for recycled paper.

For Javier and Sylvie Teixidor

Contents

Foreword

Aviad Kleinberg

Brian Stock, winner of the Feltrinelli prize for the combined fields of history and literature for 2007, has been studying the relationship between men, ideas, and texts for more than three decades, from his fascinating study of Bernard Silvester, *Myth and Science in the Twelfth Century: A Study of Bernard Silvester* (1972) to the present volume.

In his first published work, Stock examines the work of an until-then almost forgotten writer, Bernard Silvester. Silvester, he argues, can teach us something important about intellectual change and its historical setting. In a world dominated by Neoplatonism, Silvester proclaimed himself a Platonist, but this Platonist reversed the priorities of Platonism. He viewed the phenomena of nature as the starting point for true knowledge and what we call platonic forms or ideas and the knowledge that comes from contemplating them as secondary. He did this in concert with a number of other thinkers of that period, like Thierry of Chartres, who were convinced that in order to understand nature you must study the material world. These people were always called "Platonists," but in fact that term must be understood in a very different way from what we usually understand by it. This, then, was subversive thinking—filling old intellectual wine skins with new wine. Twelfth-century thinkers sought ways to legitimize the concrete, the material. But this paradigm shift (to borrow a term from Thomas Kuhn) from otherworldly to worldly attitudes had to be done while denying its radical implications.

Symbolically this subversive thinking was expressed by the reappearance of "pagan" myths. Stock notes that one finds in the twelfth century a renewed interest in personification, which comes up through Claudian and a number of ancient writers, like Prudentius and Boethius, in which there was a classical tradition of seeing the gods as personifications of forces or ideas and of making these ideas speak and act as persons in their own names. But in the Middle Ages such literary or philosophical myths didn't mean quite what they meant to late ancient authors who were still working within what we would call "Classical Mythology." One of the things that was notably different was the introduction of history into myth—the notion that these deities were human products with a history, something that classical authors, of course, do not talk about at all. History in the twelfth century was paradoxically not a thing of the past, but a very present force. Like science, it expressed the determination of thinkers to examine their world from the vantage point of the concrete and the present—the here and the now.

Also new was the personification of emotions. In the twelfth century such personifications become very important. There was a very interesting reorientation of the question of human action towards human passion—again a shift from the universal and timeless to the fully contextualized connection of body and soul. Through people like Bernard Silvester, science entered the picture. There are things called "Natural Laws," notes Bernard, and God invented them. But once he put them in place they just run on their own. He doesn't interfere in them. If you want to understand the world, then, look around you.

In his next major study, *The Implications of Literacy: Written Language and Models of Interpretation in the Twelfth Century* (1983), Stock's interest shifts from the history of ideas to the process of creating and facilitating ideas in their social context. To understand what made possible the immense intellectual changes of the twelfth century, Stock developed the notion of "textual communities"—communities made of both reading and nonreading members, organized around real or imaginary "root texts." In the West, Stock notes, there has never been a total separation of the oral and the written spheres. In each sphere there was a striving for equilibrium, based not on what individuals do, but on what happens in disciplines, languages, different dimensions of the culture.

The textual community, according to Stock, was the fundamental motor of social change in Christian society. In the eleventh and twelfth centuries the deep demographic and economic developments required the formation of new modes of thought and new modes of social organization. Literacy was both a supply that expanded in response to growing demand—merchants and administrators, for example—and a mechanism of social change. It was a unique phenomenon, one that didn't exist in the ancient world. The structural changes in medieval society were probably the most important factor, but there were others—certain kinds of eschatological thinking in Christian society: for example, seeing the future as a justification for radical action in the present. Eschatology was in the air and it influenced illiterate as well as literate people. It also made familiarity with ostensibly irrelevant texts seem relevant and even urgent. The changes were a convergence, a coming together of sometimes contradictory forces and people from very different backgrounds that one would expect to produce very different agendas.

The new social, cultural, and religious agendas that suddenly began to emerge were not, as some historians claim, just expressions of social economic and political interests. They reflected a serious reworking of some of the fundamental teachings of Scriptures: for example, the notion of progressive grace, that achieving salvation begins in this world and continues to the next. That this reworking was taking place at this particular moment is due to changes in the infrastructure, but it had a life of its own that went beyond class interest.

The great controversy about the Eucharist, whether the bread and wine on the altar are the "real" flesh and blood of Jesus Christ, is a case in point. If Christ is not just a memory or a symbol but a real presence, then that presence, which is created by a communal act—the partaking of communion—must be operating in the world through the community. That is a tremendous motive for rethinking Man and the World, to use Burkhardt's definition of the Italian Renaissance.

Stock shows how communities function in a multilayered universe, where individual and social self-examination plays an important role in shaping identity. Communities act and constantly reflect upon their actions. As he observes in his collection of essays, *Listening for the Text: On the Uses of the Past* (1990): "Action is 'social' insofar as its subjectively organized understanding takes account of the behavior of others and is interrelated with it."

This awareness of the reflective aspect of every human society and the Western choice to make texts the privileged means of taking account of the behavior of others, and indeed of the world, has led Stock to a reexamination of the works of St. Augustine of Hippo, who perhaps more than anyone else influenced Western attitudes toward reading and textual interpretation. In his major study, *Augustine the Reader: Meditation, Self-Knowledge and the Ethics of Interpretation* (1996), Stock examines the hermeneutics of the bishop of Hippo and its profound influence on Western letters, Western theology, and Western psychology.

Augustine offered a culture a new theory of reading, of what texts do, which made texts the center of communal being. According to Stock, Augustine represents a watershed in Western approaches to reading and self-knowledge because of the identification he created between the philosopher and the reader. Ancient philosophers, particularly those in the Platonic tradition up to Plotinus, were suspicious of the value of reading, especially literary texts, for the attainment of self-knowledge. They believed in the primacy of the spoken word and live dialogue. But Augustine established reading as the fundamental tool for both the acquisition of knowledge and the betterment of the self. This Augustinian approach to reading emerged to a large extent as a result of his philosophy of language: asserting that the words we use cannot convey the true realities, Augustine was highly skeptical of the ability of discursive reason to reach certain truths, and therefore insisted that only through the reading and interpretation of the Word of God manifested in time—Holy Scriptures—can we can attain certain knowledge about the created world and self. In addition, his assertion that we grasp meaning only by means of the flow of sequences of words taking place in time also led him to reason that the understanding of the meaning of each and every individual life requires us to evaluate the succession of events that make up this life. The reading of one's own personal history retained in memory—and the writing of the autobiography—thus becomes for Augustine a crucial aspect of our attempt to understand who we are.

While emphasizing the seminal role that reading the Bible and our own book of memory serves in the quest for self-knowledge, Augustine also stressed the value of reading as a spiritual exercise that allows us to shape and transform the self. As Stock argues, reading—both oral and silent— was never an autonomous activity for Augustine, but went hand in hand with meditation (*meditatio*). Augustine holds that the act of reading allows us to concentrate the senses on an inner object and thus to create the "psychological precondition for meditative experience." Reading provides the material for reflection that dominates the accompanying meditation, whether in the form of the divine precepts of conduct contained in the biblical text, or by facilitating a comparison between the narrative of the self as it was and the self as it should be. Both of these activities taken together allow us to fashion the "new man" in the Pauline sense, to forget the old self and shape the new one in light of the ideal presented in Scripture. Thus, in Stock's reading, Augustine's notion of reflectivity does not lead to isolation, but to social action, as the bishop's own career manifests. The recurrent Augustinian revivals in the West (reaching a high point in the Reformation) are expressions of the western tendency to transform meditation into action.

But the story is not straightforward; nor is it simple. In his collection of essays *After Augustine: The Meditative Reader and the Text* (2001), Stock examines the impact on the West of Augustine's theory of reading, from late antiquity to the Renaissance, and, as ever, offers his readers a combination of original insight and impressive erudition. The medieval West, as Stock shows, retained the Augustinian emphasis on the essential literary nature of our experience of the self (self-awareness has much in common with the interpretation of a text), as well as on the value of the practices of reading and writing for the ethical formation of the self. Medieval hagiographies, as Stock shows, continued to emphasize the value of stories for the transformation of readers by providing narratives depicting the lives of saints in historical time. Monastic circles, moreover, developed the Augustinian use of reading as an ascetic practice—that is, as a mechanism for transforming the reader—as is evident in the prevalence of the practices of *lectio divina* and *lectio spiritualis* in the Middle Ages. The impact of the Augustinian literary approach to the self is apparent in the proliferation of autobiographical writings in the Augustinian revival that began in the eleventh and twelfth centuries. Nonetheless, Stock argues, while the authors of the period, such as Peter Abelard and Guibert of Nogent, drew upon the Augustinian model of self-writing, they also transformed it by giving in their works a much larger role to intentionality and to the moral responsibility of individuals for their actions and fates.

From the fourteenth century onward, Stock observes, we witness the end of the era in the history of reading that began with Augustine. The growth of silent reading as a result of the rise in literacy during the period brought to an end the separation between reading aloud and the silent meditation that followed it, and thus led to a decline in the contemplative aspect of reading. In addition, the emergence of humanistic practices of reading, which stressed the analytical rather than ethical uses of texts, also contributed to the decline in the employment of reading for ethical purposes. Finally, the general weakening of the authority of sacred ontologies of the period led to growing skepticism about the ability of reading and writing to fashion ethically informed selves, as is evident in the works of Petrarch, Montaigne, and Thomas More. This skepticism ultimately led to

Descartes's distrust of book learning and his return to the ancient reliance on reason alone as the foundation of philosophical inquiry. What we have lost because of all these developments, argues Stock, is the late antique and medieval ability to form a close relationship between ethics and literature and to promote reading as a contemplative practice that leads to self-reflection and to ethical action.

This book is based on Brian Stock's Jerusalem Lectures in History in Memory of Menahem Stern, hosted by the Historical Society of Israel, delivered in Jerusalem in April 2005. In lecture after lecture, Stock reviews the past and confronts it with new texts and new ideas. It was a pleasure to listen to his lectures; but one suspects that the author expects his texts to be read and reflected upon, for the old ideas and insights, he believes, have not become obsolete. They are worthy of further thought. This foreword has led you to the threshold, but you're on your own from this point on. Read this book, it might change your mind.

Preface

I would like to express my gratitude to the Historical Society of Israel for the privilege of delivering the Menahem Stern Jerusalem Lectures in 2005. I am especially indebted to Michael Heyd and Zvi Yekutiel for their hospitality during my period of residence in Jerusalem. I thank Mrs. Dalit Danenberg for the time she devoted to coordinating my activities and arranging visits to historical sites.

I am equally grateful to Aviad Kleinberg and Yaarah Bar On for their companionship over many years and for their helpful introduction to the different cultures, peoples, and regions of Israel. I thank Moshe Idel for his warm reception at the Institute for Advanced Judaic Studies in the Shalom Hartman Institute, as well as for many conversations on topics of mutual interest to Judaism and Christianity. I am mindful of the time taken on my behalf by Ora Limor, Yousef Kaplan, and Guy and Sarah Strousma. I should also like to acknowledge the generosity of my Dominican friends at the École Biblique et Archéologique Française, who permitted me the use their excellent library.

These lectures are printed as they were delivered with the addition of notes, where necessary, and supporting texts that could not be discussed owing to limitations of time. In preparing the text for publication I have benefited from conversations with Brad Inwood, Robin Jackson, Aviad Kleinberg,

Preface

John Magee, Carlo Ossola, Domenico Pietropaulo, Nancy Regalado, and Paul Saenger. Peter Brown kindly drew my attention to the little-known accounts of sacred reading in Coptic and Syriac texts that are quoted in chapter 2. I am deeply indebted to Maruja Jackman for reading the completed manuscript and to Bill Edwards and Caroline Suma for their invaluable bibliographical assistance at the library of the Pontifical Institute of Mediaeval Studies.

Toronto, 2006

ETHICS THROUGH LITERATURE

I   The Reader's Dilemma

No man was ever yet a great poet, without being at the
same time a profound philosopher.
—Samuel Taylor Coleridge, *Biographia Literaria*

I

The topic of these lectures is the relationship between ethics, reading, and the creative imagination
in Western culture. The discussions are organized
around a pair of concepts that have a lengthy tradition in
reflection on the subject, namely the "ascetic" and "aesthetic" approaches to reading. I would like to begin by de-
fining what I mean by these terms. This can be done by
means of a brief review of the well-known statements on the
teaching of ethics through literature by two early figures in
the field, Plato and Augustine of Hippo.

In books 3 and 10 of the *Republic*, Socrates questions the
usefulness of imaginative literature, chiefly epic and drama,
in the ethical training of the guardians in his ideal commonwealth. He accuses poetry of moral improprieties, claiming
that Homer, in his stories about the gods, frequently relates
things that could never have taken place. In Socrates' view
there are only two types of stories, true and false. Homer's
mostly fall under the rubric of *pseudos*, which means "lying,
falsehood, fraud, or deceit" but can be translated on occasion
in the *Republic* as "fiction." What Socrates and Plato have
in mind is the elimination from the guardians' classroom of
"all works of the imagination, all fictitious narratives . . . in
myth or allegory, fable or parable, poetry or romance."[1]

In book 10, where a more general summary of this position is presented, it is proposed that poets, like painters, deal with appearances rather than realities. Poetry is called a type of imitation (*mimesis*), in which a picture is colored, so to speak, "with words and phrases."[2] Plato does not rule out the aesthetic appreciation of literary or artistic creations, but in his view the knowledge arising from these endeavors is always approximate.[3] No matter how skillfully a work of art is brought into being, its design can offer no evidence that its author possesses a genuine understanding of the realities on which it is based, which consist in forms. Lacking this knowledge, literature that purports to deal with ethical issues, as do Homer's stories, cannot be said to rest on a reliable foundation. Plato concludes that it is by means of a rational methodology, rather than through the rhetorical devices of imaginative literature, that ethical behavior is to be established in his commonwealth.

Augustine transforms Plato's arguments in books 1 and 3 of the *Confessions*,[4] where he offers the readers of his autobiography a criticism of ancient epic and drama in a Christian context. He too is convinced of the immoral character of the tales about the pagan deities,[5] and he echoes Plato's statements concerning poetic images as appearances. But he is less concerned with the realities that may lie behind such images than with the rhetorical power of literary performances to create a false source for emotions. As a schoolboy, he recalls, he memorized and recited lengthy passages from the *Aeneid*:

I was forced to learn about the wanderings of some legendary fellow named Aeneas (forgetful of my own wanderings) and to weep over the death of a Dido who took her own life because of unrequited love. While I was reading this, I was myself dying, so to speak, by my alienation from God, but my miserable condition brought no tears to my eyes.[6]

The Reader's Dilemma

Commenting on the educational value of poetry two decades later in *The City of God*, the bishop of Hippo reiter-
ates this view, remarking that "Vergil . . . is the best and
most renowned of all poets, and for this reason he is read by
children at an early age—they take great draughts of his poetry into their unformed minds."[7]

A variant of this complaint is found in book 3 of the
Confessions, where Augustine recalls his attraction for the
theater during his student days in Carthage. He asks why
"a person should wish to experience suffering by watch-
ing grievous and tragic events which he would not wish to
endure?" His answer is that such a person "wants to suf-
fer the pain given by being a spectator of these sufferings,
and the pain itself is his pleasure." In contrast to Aristotle, who argues in favor of a cathartic release of emotions
by means of tragedy, thus detaching the feelings of the audience from those of the actors,[8] Augustine is convinced
that the audience is caught up in the real emotions generated by the drama, even while knowing that their source
is fictional. "The more anyone is moved by these scenes,"
he observes, "the less free he is from similar passions. . . .
The greater his pain, the greater his approval of the actor in
these representations."[9]

Plato and Augustine are talking about a contrast between
a literary culture that offers entertainment and one that
promotes moral improvement. At the center of this discussion is the status of what is imagined—whether what is perceived is accurately understood and interpreted in the mind
and, if not, whether this is a cause for moral concern. Plato
is indirectly criticizing the teaching methods of fourth-
century Athens, which included the rote memorization of
lengthy passages from Homer, Hesiod, and the dramatists.[10]
Augustine suggests that little had changed in this aspect of
education by the fourth century A.D.,[11] and agrees with Plato

3

on the weaknesses of secular literature for teaching ethics. Socrates sums up the position of both writers in book 3 of the *Republic*, after quoting a number of passages that preface accounts of irregular behavior and unbridled emotions among the deities in the *Iliad* and *Odyssey*: "Not that they lack poetic merit," he says of these stories, "or that they don't give pleasure to most people, . . . but if our young men take these kinds of things seriously, then it is hardly likely that any of them will think twice of behaving like this." In Plato's view, what the guardians as well as the general population of the commonwealth should hope to gain from their education is a defensible ethical outlook. But "if we want the young to develop self-discipline," Socrates concludes, "I don't think these are the right things for them to hear—though it is no surprise if they are entertaining in other ways."[12]

Two questions can be asked about these statements against the teaching of ethics through literature. The first is whether Plato and Augustine consistently follow their own advice. The answer would seem to be no. Plato discredits epic and drama as guides for moral education but introduces a literary vehicle of his own, the rational dialogue, which is less imagistic than Homer but entertaining in other ways. Augustine tells the story of his rejection of such mythological narratives in an equally original literary genre, the confessional autobiography. In short, both have left us works of high art, and these are responses to recognizable models: Plato looks back to the dramatists for inspiration, while Augustine, following Vergil, writes a type of epic in which the hero does not abandon a fallen Troy but attempts to abandon the fallen and sinful person that he no longer wants to be. Both argue that mimesis is responsible for the critical weakness in imaginative literature, since art cannot repro-

4

duce reality; yet, in making their respective cases, both re-appropriate the very literary methods that they are arguing against. This involves imitation of earlier literary genres, drama and epic, by later ones, dialogue and autobiography. In each the imitation is unfaithful, not, I would argue, in order to illustrate the unreliability of such an approach, but to tell us why the teaching of ethics by means of literature cannot do without it.

Within this series of mimetic reproductions, moreover, the readers of the *Republic* and the *Confessions* are not asked to choose between "ascetic" and "aesthetic" alternatives: the one is advocated in support of the other, literature acting in the service of philosophy in Plato and theology in Augustine. We have to conclude that the ethical objective, which is the announced intention of both authors, is reinforced and somewhat undermined by their differing but curiously similar commitment to what Roland Barthes called "the pleasure of the text." This is the source of the reader's dilemma: the paradoxical situation in Western reading history in which the aesthetic alternative, which is initially rejected as being sensory, material, ephemeral, or superficial, is invariably enlisted in support of an ascetic program.

The second question that can be asked about Plato and Augustine in a discussion about this aspect of reading concerns their respective situations in the history of the subject. We want to know whether they are talking about the same issues in the field, and here again the answer is negative. Plato does not discuss reading very much, whereas Augustine talks at length about a number of types of reading—factual, mystical, and interpretive. Also, what they have to say on the topic differs considerably. When Plato refers to texts, his words require an explanation; an example is *Phaedrus* 274b–278e, his well-known "critique of writing."

What he means by this important but difficult passage cannot be understood without drawing on statements concerning writing, reading, and the philosophy of mind elsewhere in his works.[13] By contrast, Augustine's observations on the experience of texts in books 1 and 3 of the *Confessions* are straightforward: they can be corroborated but not better explained by what he says on the subject elsewhere, for example in books 1 to 3 of *De Doctrina Christiana*. His reflections come at the end of some four centuries of continuous circulation of literary texts in the Roman world,[14] and, like Jerome's observations on book culture from the same decades, they synthesize thinking on the subject in a manner that offers guidance for the Middle Ages and the Renaissance.[15]

Plato's reluctance to talk about reading and Augustine's openness are not only reflections of different styles and attitudes; they also tell us something about the stages of the ancient conceptualization of the reading process. Thinking on the subject was just beginning to take shape in Plato's day,[16] but had reached a period of consolidation in Augustine's. The bishop of Hippo is the first genuine theorist in the field; "theory" in this sense being understood as a bringing together and recombination of many things that had been said previously in different places in the disciplines of grammar and rhetoric. In view of the early phase in the subject's development that Plato represents, he is less certain than Augustine concerning what can be gained from reading, as contrasted with the well-established art of conversing or dialoguing. True, in the *Republic*, the guardians are taught moral lessons by means of simplified narratives that are read to them, but this storytelling is conceived as a preparation for something higher, namely philosophy. By contrast, in the *Confessions* Augustine claims for reading, and for reading alone, the analytical capacity for dealing with different genres of moral instruction, including poetry, mythology, philosophy, and scripture. What was most valuable in his childhood education, after learning to speak, was learning to read. "On that foundation," he notes, "I have acquired the faculty . . . of being able to peruse whatever I find written and to write myself whatever I wish."[17]

2

According to Plato and Augustine, then, we can think of the ascetic approach to literature as being concerned with an ethical objective that lies beyond the aesthetic appreciation of the text. By contrast, the aesthetic approach is one that chiefly involves the pleasure of the text in and for itself.

The remainder of this lecture is conceived as an introduction to this subject, which I discuss by means of a "topos"[18] that I call "the scene of reading" as it arises in the writings of Abelard, Dante, and Virginia Woolf. In lectures 2 and 3 I turn to ascetic and aesthetic readership as separate issues and look at some critical moments in their development.

I begin my examination of the theme with Peter Abelard (d. 1142), who is thought to have been the author of all, or nearly all, of his autobiography, which is called *Historia Calamitatum* (*The Story of My Misfortunes*).[19] In this account of his early troubles there is a well-known scene of reading in which Heloise is seduced.[20] She was about seventeen at the time—the niece of Fulbert, a canon of Notre Dame, with whom she was living and receiving her education.[21] As a logician, Abelard was then at the height of his fame. But his concern with his success, by his own subsequent admission, had got the better of his judgment. He had acquired a mixed reputation: popular among students, who crowded into his lectures, but criticized by the authorities, who condemned his treatise *The Unity and Trinity of God* (possibly on inadequate grounds) at the Council of Soissons in 1121.[22] Restless and intemperate by nature, he gradually abandoned the traditional lifestyle of a womanless scholar, devoting himself, as he put it, to *philosophia* and *sacra lectio*, and entered a period of personal incertitude. This was accompanied by nonconformist behavior by which he acquired a reputation for intellectual intolerance and imprudent amorous pursuits.[23]

He was on the lookout for potential female conquests when he heard about Heloise. Her erudition impressed him rather more than her appearance;[24] a telling detail, which helps to explain why his passion faded, as Heloise ruefully suggests,[25] and why she adapted so readily to the studious monastic life after his departure.[26] He reckoned she was easy prey: he was favored by Fortune, or so he thought at the time, since the avaricious Fulbert, in return for tutoring his niece, offered him lodgings in the house where they lived, which lay comfortably within the precincts of Notre Dame. "There is little more to say," he relates in the *Historia*:

We first came together in one house, then in one mind. Using our lessons as an occasion, we gave ourselves over entirely to love. Our eagerness for reading offered us the secrecy and privacy that love desires. Thus, while our books lay open, the words that flooded from our lips were about love rather than about what we were reading: there were more kisses than thoughts, and my hands were often led to her breasts rather than to the pages. Love more frequently turned our eyes toward each other than our reading directed them toward the text.[27]

This is a celebrated scene of reading, from which later authors benefited, including Petrarch, who may have been acquainted with Abelard's adventures.[28] The *Historia Calam-*

itatum superficially resembles Augustine's *Confessions*, inasmuch as it is a story of the conquest of pride by humility, or in Abelard's case, by humiliation. The catastrophe is the result of two cardinal sins, Abelard's pride and Fulbert's greed. But while Augustine may be the distant model for the reversal, the seduction scene has no parallel in the *Confessions* and differs in important details from Augustine's conversion by means of a book, the Epistle to the Romans, at *Confessions* 8.12.28–30.

What the two scenes have in common is the use of a book as a means to an end rather than as an end in itself, and this is typical of the topos of "the scene of reading" throughout its history. It is not the text of Paul's epistle but divine grace that permits Augustine to overcome his concupiscence, and not the contents of a propaedeutic work but the physical proximity of the readers in question that permits Abelard's moral constraint to be swept away so that emotion can triumph over reason in his seduction of Heloise. In passing from Augustine to Abelard, moreover, we move from one sort of reading to another: from the experience of one person to that of two, and from a single male speaker, who describes a permanent change in outlook, to a male and female, who give separate accounts of consequences arising from contact with a text, neither of which, as it turns out, is permanent.

Unlike Augustine's conversion in the *Confessions*, therefore, the scene of reading in the *Historia* is gendered. There is in fact not one interpretation of the episode within the text but two. The male reading is a Christian moral paradigm, which is completed when Abelard sets up the ascetic study program of the Paraclete as the antidote for the reading that accompanies the seduction, in which there is a pleasurable consequence if not an aesthetic appreciation of the text that the pair are perusing. In Heloise's mind, moreover, this type of reading experience may have been linked to another literature of pleasure, namely Abelard's *carmina amatoria*,[29] which are mentioned in the *Historia* but have not survived. These love lyrics play a role with their audience that is comparable to the theatrical performances Augustine saw in Carthage, namely the indulgence in the emotional qualities of a text for its own sake. In both cases aesthetics is contrasted with ascetics within a traditional moral scheme.

The female reading does not fit any known pattern. This troubling nonconformity may have been inserted deliberately into the *Historia* by Abelard or by his reviser, either of whom may have wished to rework the biblical connection, emphasized among others by Augustine, between femaleness and moral disorder. Thus Heloise is pictured as wanting to enjoy Abelard at once as her lover and equal, even if in the end their relationship is spiritualized by their separation and her entry into a religious community. She is also presented as desiring the benefits of his intellectual guidance at the Paraclete, just as she desired his grammatical tutoring as a young student in Paris. Abelard is thus portrayed through her eyes in two roles that are difficult to reconcile in a single person, namely lover and mentor.[30]

The "male" and "female" readings leave many questions unanswered concerning the connection between love and marriage in the correspondence. The major difficulty arises from the bookish nature of the arguments of both parties. Their statements of their views appear to be detached from the strong sentiments that accompany the initial encounter between the lovers. They read like an attempt on the part of the author or reviser of the letters to create opposed discourses of emotion and mind. This is an ancient strategy, which is seldom invoked to the female's advantage, even in the case of the abandoned Dido, who may have been in Abelard's thoughts, as she surely was in Augustine's when the latter ended his illicit love affair with his Carthaginian mistress after the birth of his son, just as, in a different context, Abelard deserted the pregnant Heloise. Ironically, Heloise criticizes this very attitude of detachment in her first letter using Seneca's epistolary model, forgetting, perhaps, that it was precisely this Stoic virtue that the elder sage wished to impart to his devoted follower and it was in search of such a method that Lucilius took up the pursuit of asceticism through reading. The *Moral Epistles* is the only ancient ethical treatise extant that is composed as a letter collection; the correspondence of Abelard and Heloise is its medieval successor, and looks forward to a long series of epistolary novels climaxed by Richardson's *Clarissa*.

In sum, the lovers' positions on marriage, although differing in content, share an academic quality, as if they arose from long hours of perusing moral, legal, and philosophical texts. While Abelard is in favor of marriage, his reasons are not very convincing when viewed in the context of his actions; and while Heloise is against it, her reasons are not persuasive either. Following many ancient writers, he downplays the value of romantic love, hardly mentioning the affair in his segment of the subsequent correspondence. He thus attempts to create the impression that in the long run it did not matter.[31] But we are not persuaded, since, in contrast to Augustine, who dismisses his mistress without so much as mentioning her name,[32] Abelard becomes the first philosopher whose moral outlook is unquestionably influenced by his experience with a woman. As for Heloise, her negativity regarding marriage is equally implausible. Her statements are based not so much on her feelings, although these surface from time to time, as on tired, antifeminist arguments from Jerome's *Contra Jovinianum*. What rings false in both cases is the increasing level of abstraction as the letters proceed: we hear less about the shame, suffering, and psychological injury brought about by the affair, and more about what books tell us that moralistic reactions to such things ought to be.

Another problem in the correspondence concerns the status of friendship, and this too is handled somewhat bookishly. The *Historia Calamitatum* is written to an unnamed friend in a classical literary genre, the *consolatio*.[33] At the moment he is thinking of her seduction, Abelard seriously contemplates a series of letters, perhaps equally consolatory, with Heloise. Yet, in her response to reading the *Historia* (which, let us note, is conveyed by friends rather than sent by Abelard),[34] she is not impressed by the suggestion of a postcoital exchange, in which a passionate affair would be rendered as a passionless text. True, she quotes Seneca to the effect that letters are like absent friends, but she does not suggest that they can replace Abelard's physical presence. This is what she is trying to say but finds hard to say, since, no less than he, she can express her emotions only through a filter of erudition. In the end she deploys her learning cleverly but unpersuasively. But not entirely so, since, as she speaks, the reader has the impression that the contrivances that litter Abelard's autobiography are being taken up, played with, and finally jettisoned. The message that comes through is that love triumphs over friendship, at least over friendship mediated by texts.

Heloise's letters, then, are innovative on the topics of marriage and friendship, but do not resolve all the issues they raise, nor, in my view, do they intend to do so. The same can be said for her fictionalizing, which is still another bookish feature of the correspondence, also introduced for moral pur-

poses. Heloise accuses Abelard of fashioning an ascetic utopia in the wilderness; afterward, of leaving her and her sis-
ters at the Paraclete in order to tend "another's vineyard."[35]
Despite the benefits of the spiritual life, she refuses to give
up the original image of her lover, which may have dated
from before their meeting, as did Abelard's image of her:

What king or philosopher could match your fame? What district,
town or village did not long to see you? . . . Every wife, every young
girl desired you in your absence and was on fire in your presence;
queens and great ladies envied me my joys and my bed.[36]

It is the portrait of the romantic and rationalist Abelard,
popular in France in the nineteenth century, that persists
in our minds when we have finished the correspondence,
rather than the more accurate picture of the aged, disillu-
sioned philosopher described by Peter the Venerable, who
withdraws into a life of piety and otherworldliness at Cluny
just before his death.[37] And it is the portrayal of Heloise,
as committed to this static image rather than to the his-
torically evolving Abelard, that may be the final irony of
the letters, suggesting as it does, between the lines, the sor-
didness of stereotypical medieval romance. In the end this
powerful letter collection leaves us, perhaps by design, asking whether Heloise's behavior vindicates the Platonic/Au-
gustinian position against imaginative literature, which
is so carefully implanted into the texts, or whether we are
hearing a genuinely new female voice, which is difficult to
classify by means of ancient models.

My second illustration of a scene of reading from the Middle
Ages is the story of Paolo and Francesca from *Inferno*, canto
5, in Dante's *Divina Commedia*.

In the scholarly interpretation of this canto, which has changed considerably over the past two centuries,[38] no one has suggested that the *Historia Calamitatum* was a substantive source of the celebrated episode in which the lovers meet their death. Yet the story is comparable to the seduction of Heloise in two respects. The account is based on historical events, and the downfall of the female protagonist is brought about through reading.

Francesca (or Franceschina) da Rimini, the heroine of canto 5, was unhappily betrothed to Gianno Ciotto or Gian Ciotto Malatesta, lord of Rimini, as part of an agreement for settling a dispute between their fathers, Guido da Polenta and Malatesta da Riminio, shortly after 1275. Guido feared that his beautiful, independent-minded daughter would refuse a match with the unattractive and unmannerly Gianno Ciotto. In order to overcome her opposition he arranged for her to see Paolo, his more presentable brother, whom she allegedly mistook for his sibling and agreed to wed. The union produced a daughter, Concordia (not mentioned in canto 5), and Francesca was later able to join Paolo, presumably without the knowledge of his own wife, the contessa di Ghaggiolo, or their two sons. When the illicit relationship was discovered by Gianno Ciotto, he intended to murder only Paolo but accidentally killed Francesca as well. The crime occurred sometime between 1283 and 1286, after which Gianno Ciotto remarried, dying around 1300.

It is possible that Dante, then resident in Florence, became acquainted with Paolo Malatesta between February 1282 and 1283, when the latter was *capitano del popolo*. His familiarity with Paolo and his family may be responsible for the sympathy that is shown toward the hapless sinners, for whom he displays considerable pity even if he does not suggest forgiveness. Later, when he composed the *Paradiso* in Ravenna, Dante was the guest of another member of Francesca's family, Guido Novello da Polenta. By this time *Inferno* canto 5 had been published and possibly read by some of her relatives, who would have been pleased by his generous portrait of the lovers. Dante lends support to this interpretation by creating an insider's perspective on the introduction of Paolo and Francesca in canto 5. In contrast to the accounts of the unrepentant sinners of antiquity mentioned by Vergil, for whom a minimum of historical details are supplied for the reader's benefit, virtually no context is provided for the tragic couple that plays the principal role. Dante evidently assumes that the contemporary reader knows something about Francesca already, since she is identified only through an allusion to her place of origin "on the river Po," namely Ravenna (v. 98).

As in the case of Abelard's *Historia Calamitatum*, which is the sole literary witness to his love affair with Heloise, Dante's account is the main source of information concerning the sins of adultery and murder related in verses 82–143 of *Inferno* 5. Later retellings of the story are based on the narrative in the *Commedia*, including the influential interpretation of Boccaccio.[39] Although their misfortunes are rarely compared by medieval writers, Heloise and Francesca subsequently become archetypes for tragic heroines in French and Italian literature, reappearing respectively in Rousseau's epistolary novel *La nouvelle Héloïse* (1761) and Gabriele d'Annunzio's play *Francesca da Rimini* (1902).

At the point in their journey at which the story begins, Dante and Vergil have descended to the second circle of the *inferno*, where Minos, the mythical king of Crete, notorious for cruelty, sits in judgment on unrepentant sinners:

> . . . i peccator carnali,
> che la ragion sommettono al talento (vv. 38–39).

[carnal sinners, who subject reason to desire or passion].

These spirits are driven about and tormented on the winds of a perpetual storm. Their numbers include many ancient celebrities, chiefly women, among them Semiramis, queen of Assyria, accused of lust, murder, and incest; Dido, not at first mentioned by name but recognizable through her suicide; Cleopatra, who conquered Egypt through Julius Caesar, seduced Marc Anthony, and died with him after the battle of Actium; and of course Helen, daughter of Leda and Zeus and wife of Menelaus, whose abduction by Paris brought about the Trojan War. This catalogue of well-known figures acts as a background for the story of Paolo and Francesca, proceeding, so to speak, from *antiqui* to *moderni*.

Vergil enumerates *le donne antiche e' cavalieri*, succinctly presenting the reasons for their glamour and notoriety for his companion's benefit, and Dante expresses pity for these unfortunate lovers (v. 72). While he reflects on their adventures, his attention is diverted to a pair of spirits, as yet unidentified, which seem to be carried together on the raging winds that whirl back and forth in this circle of the *inferno*. The two form part of a subgroup, including Dido, which consists of lovers who not only were victims of unruly passions but presumably erred in search of more enduring sentiments. Moreover, unlike the ancient lovers, who appear individually, they come onstage as a couple, united in expression and movement. We later learn that their inability to withstand the storm's fury stands for their lack of resistance to their common passion.

On seeing them, Dante utters an affectionate greeting (*l'affettuoso grido*), while Paolo and Francesca remain motionless, hovering above him at a point in the air at which the eternally howling winds are momentarily quiet (v. 96). This is an instant of great poetic beauty in the canto, when Dante employs an image used by Vergil at *Aeneid* 5.213–

216 in order to compare the tormented lovers to a pair of doves:

> Quali colombe dal disio chiamate,
>   con l'ali alzate e ferme al dolce nido
>   vegnon per l'aere dal voler portate.
>
> [As doves, summoned by desire, come with wings poised and motionless to the sweet nest, borne by their will through the air.][40]

The story of Paolo and Francesca thus begins with contrasting images of carnal and spiritual love (vv. 90–93). Francesca then alludes to the story by which she and Paolo met their death, hinting at the contemporary significance of the episode for Dante, who for his part appears eager to engage in conversation with the two unhappy shades. She reminds him of the strength of her love for Paolo by means of a phrase used by the Florentine poets of the *stil nuovo* in his generation:

> Amor, ch'al cor gentil ratto s'apprende (v. 100)
>
> [love, which is quickly kindled in a gentle heart].

Her point is that love, once aroused, deserts no one, as the Italian writers whom Dante has in mind frequently pointed out. Her reference distinguishes Dante, who began his career as just such a love poet, from his guide, whose reputation rests on the genres of pastoral and epic. The reader likewise gains insight into the part played by Dido, who prefigures Francesca as a tragic victim of love's attraction. Vergil's pity at her fate forms a backdrop for Dante's compassion at the ignoble end that has befallen Francesca's noble soul. Accordingly, it is Vergil who tells him to ask the pair to approach. They do so, borne by their love for each other: *per quello amor che i mena . . .* (v. 78).

17

If the ethical situation of these lovers superficially invites comparison to that of Abelard and Heloise, therefore,
in Dante greater emphasis is placed on the value of love for
its own sake and on the unconquerable nature of its passion.
In the *Historia Calamitatum*, immature love brings about
separation, whereas in canto 5, two souls, condemned for
wrongs, are permanently united by a bond of love. According to Christian teachings, their sin has been brought about
by intentions as well as actions; and yet, knowing this, they
are unable to overcome the force that inspired the misdeeds
and abandon the love they once passionately enjoyed. Dante,
who places them in the *inferno*, does not suggest that their
wrongs merit anything but condemnation. Yet, as a mortal,
he cannot help but be moved by Francesca's statement of her
emotional imprisonment:

> Amor, ch'a nullo amato amar perdona,
> mi prese del costui piacer sì forte,
> che, come vedi, ancor non m'abbandona. (vv. 103–105)

> [Love, which frees no one who is loved
> from loving, took hold of me
> with such force that, as you see,
> it has not yet abandoned me.]

Another point of comparison between Heloise and Francesca arises from their similar treatment within the conven-
tional morality of their respective societies. They are condemned for permitting emotion to overcome reason, which
classical philosophy and Christianity both forbid. Yet, in
sharing this fate, they are aware that enduring love between
man and woman is beyond or above reason. As a consequence, its rationale and significance have to be sought elsewhere: possibly in the reason of emotion itself, as Romantic
poets, reinterpreting these episodes, will propose. Dante is

The Reader's Dilemma

as moved by Francesca's story as he must have been when he first learned about the pair's murder. When she has finished, he exclaims:

> "Francesca, i tuoi martiri
> a lacrimar mi fanno tristo e pio . . ." (vv. 116–117)
>
> [Francesca, your martyrdoms make me sad
> and full of pity to the point of tears.]

At this point in the canto he asks her how their desires were first aroused, in contrast to the manner in which the story is told in Abelard's *Historia*, where the narrator is chiefly preoccupied with the motivation for sinning and its consequences. In her response Francesca omits any reference to the historical circumstances—the feudal quarrel that gave rise to her marriage—and begins her account with the role of *amor* (a dim recollection, perhaps, of Dante's own experience in the *Vita Nuova*, when he first sees Beatrice). There is no uncertainty concerning the emotion in question: the word *amor* is reiterated at the beginning of three successive *terzine* (vv. 100–108), which speak in turn of Paolo's love for her, her love for him, and their joint fate as lovers.

Dante is visibly affected by her speech and withdraws so deeply into reflection that Vergil asks, "*Che pense?*" (v. 111). His response is an introduction to the reading scene that follows:

> Quando rispuosi, cominciai; "O lasso,
> quanti dolci pensier, quanto disio
> menò costoro al doloroso passo!" (vv. 113–115)
>
> [When I replied, I began: "Alas, how many sweet
>   thoughts,
> how great a desire, brought them to this grievous pass!"]

19

On this view, it was *pensier*, generated separately within, that gave rise to the emotional turmoil resulting in their deaths. The central event of the episode was not brought about by an external act, as in the case of Augustine's readerly conversion, or by an internal one, as in Abelard's seduction of Heloise. Nor are we dealing with the contents of texts. In Augustine, as noted, the book in question is a means to an end, not a text that is subjected to analysis; and, in the *Historia Calamitatum*, the reader is not told what text Abelard and Heloise are poring over together— possibly something unconnected with the topic of love.

In canto 5, however, the text is named, it is known to Dante's readers, and its content is relevant. The postreading experience, by which both parties imagine what is going to take place between them, is an imitation of the story they are reading and occurs in advance of the act itself, as if the narrative were playing a role in the intentional design; and as Dante relates the scene, it is that state of affairs, in which both minds are silently engaged with each other before a passionate embrace takes place, that effectively seals their fate, rather than their later discovery by Francesca's husband. Gianno Ciotto, hidden from view, has also enacted an internal narrative, although not one based on reading. As he observes what is taking place, he is presumably motivated by the illicit emotions of hatred and jealousy, and bent on the sin of murder.

Dante, who has remained silent, respectful, and attentive while Francesca has been speaking, now asks her for an explanation of the couple's downfall. In his view this is a sin made more damnable by combining an act of adultery and the consequence of fratricide. It is important to pay attention to the language in which this question is framed: how and by what situation (*a che e come*) love (or Love) made it possible (*concedette amore*) that they might become acquainted with their questionable desires.[41] For here again, as in the model of the topos set up by Augustine, it is not the book that is the causal force in question, but Love, which uses the book for its purposes.

She replies that one afternoon she and Paolo were reading the story of the medieval Lancelot, who was frustrated by his unfulfilled love for Guinevere, the wife of King Arthur. They were alone, simply reading for pleasure (*per diletto*, v. 127). As they read, they looked into each other's eyes and their faces reddened, as each reflected on their unhappy separation. They were overcome at the point in the text at which a heroic embrace ends the longing of the enamored Lancelot:

> Soli eravamo e sanza alcun sospetto.
> Per più fiate li occhi ci sospinse
> quella lettura, e scolorocci il viso;
> ma solo un punto fu quel che ci vinse. (vv. 129–132)

> [We were alone, without any misgiving. Many times
> that reading brought us into contact with each other and
> changed the colour of our faces: but it was only at one
> point that we were entirely overcome.]

This was the moment in the text when Lancelot, having loved Guinevere faithfully over a long period, asked for a reward, and she kissed him on his lips. Reading no further, they too fell into each other's arms, where they were surprised by her husband.

Francesca tells this touching story and recalls the trembling Paolo, as he kissed her for the first time:

> . . . la bocca mi baciò tutto tremante. . . . (v. 136)

The spirit of Paolo weeps, since he too has been silently reliving the scene; and Dante, unable to control his sympathy for the pair, falls down, as if fainting. Here he reflects the reaction of his readers, who cannot help but feel a similar compassion for the unfortunate lovers, who, like Abelard and Heloise, have been victimized by their sins of passion as well as by the sin of seeking revenge.

However, once again some aspects of this scene of reading distinguish it from the comparable episode in Abelard and place it at an even further distance from the reading lessons in Plato and Augustine. This takes place first in the use of dialogue. Dante and Vergil enter the second circle of the *inferno* in conversation. When they encounter Paolo and Francesca, the two initially speak as one; then Francesca speaks for both but seems to address Vergil and Dante separately, reminding Vergil of a Boethian adage on the sentiment of happiness during misfortune,[42] but recalling for Dante significant events in his own lifetime, some of which Vergil does not know. This double dialogue is an indication of a distinction Dante is making between *antiqui* and *moderni*: between the unrepentant lovers of the distant past, whose tragic ends are known through myth and history, and those in his own time, who are victims of feudal customs and male injustice.

The double dialogue based on historical distance is the introduction to the scene of reading, in which Paolo and Francesca enter into conversation. In this scene, as in the earlier examples of the topos, the act of reading, that is, the sound of the words read, provides a catalyst for emotion. But whereas the aesthetic reading in the *Confessions* and the *Historia* is placed within an ascetic framework—the search for God in Augustine's case and the instruction of a young woman in Abelard's—Dante's scene is preceded by an oblique but unmistakable reference to purely secular literature, namely the *dolce stil nuovo*, which transformed and spiritualized earlier French lyric poetry. The transition from French to Italian (or more accurately to Florentine) is reiterated in the scene of reading, where the model text, in contrast to Augustine and Abelard, is not in Latin but in Old French.

This pair of transformations would suggest that Dante is consciously proceeding from *exempla* drawn from classical antiquity to those of the "romance" period, that is, the age characterized by the emergence of the Romance languages and their literary genres. Viewed in this perspective, it is both the situation of sinful lovers that has changed as well as the language and literary form in which they find it appropriate to express their emotions. As a consequence, the question raised by the account of Francesca in canto 5 is not that of choosing between the alternatives of tragedy *or* romance but of how one might *combine* the two in a single narrative, whose complexity is communicable only by means of a double reading. This involves the actors, Paolo and Francesca, at one level, as they read and interpret *Lancelot du lac* with their own pleasure in mind, and Dante's audience, at another, in which there is an awareness of sin and, if the circumstances were known, of impending disaster.

In Augustine and Abelard, the act of reading gives rise to enactments that take place in the world: in the one this concerns a celibate life in the priesthood, and in the other a love affair with a vulnerable younger woman. In neither does the central character complete a single mental narrative that can be said to be in his thoughts at the time that the "scene of reading" takes place. By contrast, in canto 5, the reader, following Dante's own understanding of the scene, is always aware that two narratives are simultaneously at work. Paolo and Francesca enter the scene already in love and separated by circumstances. The intentional design by which they are reunited is present in their minds when the episode in the world takes place. The second narrative, the story of Lancelot that they read together, acts as a stimulus for completing the first. Furthermore the pair are aware of what is taking place, in contrast to Augustine, who is surprised by grace, and Abelard, who, despite arrogance, cannot entirely have anticipated his successful seduction.

Paolo and Francesca thus perceive the difference between reality and fiction, that is, between the lives that that they are living and the scene that they are reading about. Theirs is a tragedy of self-consciousness, and, as a result, Plato's problem is turned around: this is not mimesis imperfectly reflecting reality but reality augmented and complemented by a troubling form of mimesis. Inasmuch as the completion is based on a personal interpretation of the story of Lancelot and Guinevere—as if, somehow, the story pertained to the lovers and was intended to be thrown their way at this moment—it represents an internal form of mimesis, interpretive in function, which is not anticipated in ancient thinking on the subject before Augustine, who understands several scenes in the *Confessions* in this fashion, including, of course, the analysis of the theater audience's response to dramatic performances in book 3, to which reference has already been made.

Dante's knowledge of the story of Lancelot and Guinevere was based on his personal reading of the twelfth-century Old French *Lancelot du lac*:[43] there he found a situation comparable to that of Paolo and Francesca, namely a secret love unknown to a third party, Galahad, who unwittingly brings the parties together (cf. v. 137). The transition from earlier to later forms of the story is free of clerical influences, which generally dominate medieval discussions of lust.[44] Lancelot and Guinevere and Paolo and Francesca are laypeople,

The Reader's Dilemma

although different in milieux. In the case of Lancelot, the guide is the chivalric code of illicit love; in the case of Paolo, it is romantic love. Dante does not accept either alternative, but envisages these contexts as the background against which a discussion of sinful love can take place.

Within the plan of the *Commedia*, moreover, Dante incorporates this instance of aesthetic reading into an ascetic design. This is the larger canvas on which all the narratives of the *Inferno* are enacted. His intention is clarified in the vision of *valore infinito* in canto 33 of the *Paradiso*. Here he returns to a model evidently inspired by Augustine: it is abounding grace that permits him a momentary vision of endless goodness, in whose depths he perceives contained, bound by love in one volume, all that is scattered about in the universe:

> Oh abbondante grazia ond'io presunsi
> ficcar lo viso per la luce etterna,
> tanto che la verduta vi consunsi!
> Nel suo profondo vidi che s'interna,
> legato con amore in un volume,
> ciò che per l'universo si squaderna.
> (canto 33, vv. 82–87)

The inspiration for this image is likely taken from *Confessions* 13.15.18, where Augustine uses the metaphor of the book to describe the integrating power of the Word of God. In paradise, the bishop of Hippo proposes, the angels do not read in words and syllables, but in the intentions of God: "They read, they choose, they love. They ever read, and what they read never passes away. . . . Their codex is never closed, nor is their book ever folded shut. For you yourself are a book to them. . . ."[45] In the *Commedia* this overarching text forms part of *l'amor che move il sole e l'altre stelle* (canto 33, v. 145).

25

3

The reassuring picture of the reading process found in the writings of Augustine, Abelard, and Dante is somewhat problematized during the Renaissance. Two of the figures who contribute significantly to the change in perspective are Petrarch and Montaigne, who died respectively in 1374 and 1592.

In their writings the ancient question of ambiguity in language, which lies in the background of many medieval discussions of moral issues, enters a new phase of its historical development, inasmuch as literature begins to rival philosophy as a way of exploring ethical decision-making. The relevant writings of Petrarch on the subject are the *Secretum* and *Canzoniere*. In the *Secretum*, written in stages between 1347 and 1358, the question of reading for entertainment and for moral benefit is taken up in a Latin dialogue, which is one of the medieval literary forms traditionally employed for advocating the ascetic viewpoint. By contrast, in the *Canzoniere*, Petrarch presents a large part of his discussion of ethical issues in an anthology of vernacular lyric poems. I want to look briefly at the solutions proposed in each of these works and to ask what they tell us about attitudes toward the ethics of reading.

In the *Secretum*, an important moment in Petrarch's reflections on the purposes of reading occurs near the end of book 2.[46] Franciscus, as Petrarch calls himself in the dialogue, is in conversation with Augustinus, who represents the historical Augustine. Within the framework of late medieval apocalyptic thinking, and, in Petrarch's case, within the shadow of the Black Death, the pair take up the venerable problem of whether ethics can be taught, and if so, whether it can be taught through literature. If this is possible, then moral improvement can come about through literary studies, and the stern Augustinian teachings on grace and last things will have to be modified to incorporate a progressive scheme for the soul's upward movement. In the course of their debate Augustinus repeatedly criticizes Franciscus's fascination with writing love poetry, an activity that he considers worldly, ephemeral, and unduly concerned with imaginative constructions. He recommends in its place a program of traditional spiritual exercises by which Christian moral principles can effectively be conveyed. In particular he counsels Franciscus to meditate on the meaning of his conversion to the religious life, as related in book 8 of the *Confessions*. Franciscus acknowledges the importance of this event, which the historical Petrarch had been mulling over during this period, as he periodically considered but invariably rejected entering monastic life. A copy of the *Confessions* had been presented to him by a learned monk, Dionigi da Borgo San Sepolchro, in 1333, and he had allegedly carried it with him on his celebrated ascent of Mt. Ventoux, as recorded in *Familiares* 4.1. However, in the view of most contemporary scholars, this should be considered more a symbolic than an actual journey, in which Petrarch makes a case for a secular Christian spirituality alongside the traditional forms of devotion within the church.

As a consequence, Augustinian conversion cannot be envisaged as his objective in the *Secretum*, even though the literary treatment of the theme of conversion frequently recurs in the imagery of the *Canzoniere*. In their conversation about this critical event in Augustine's life, Franciscus and Augustinus focus their attention on a related issue. This consists in the instability brought about in the individual in search of enlightenment by vacillating sensations and emotions, and the negative effect of such fluctuations on sustained thinking about the ethical life. While Augustinus suggests that Franciscus can overcome this problem by reading, memorizing, and reflecting on the wisdom of the ancients, he does not draw his examples from the Bible, as does the historical Augustine in the *Confessions*, but from the writings of classical Latin authors, chiefly Vergil, Horace, Cicero, and Seneca.

Franciscus says that he has tried this method for attaining mental discipline but that it has only been temporarily successful. As long as his eyes are focused on what he is reading, he remains in a state of tranquillity, but as soon as he closes the book in which these nuggets of wisdom are contained, his anxieties return. It is his visual attention to the page rather than the content of the texts he is reading that momentarily calms his nerves. If we look back at Augustine's attempts at quieting his emotions through reading in the *Confessions*, Franciscus would seem to be practicing the first stage of the meditative process as the bishop of Hippo understands it, which is concerned with the perceptual dimension of reading. He omits the second stage, in which the mind detaches itself from the sensory impressions created by the text and explores inner meaning based on the duration of spoken words in the memory, which Augustine calls *distentio animi*.[47]

It is therefore Franciscus's technique of reading that is at fault. But so, by implication, is Augustinus's technique of reading Petrarch's lyric poems. In both cases, there is a failure to achieve permanent intellectual sustenance from impermanent graphic signs. In the light of these difficulties Augustinus attempts a generalization concerning erudite reading practices in the fourteenth century. In his view, these have given rise to a good deal of hypothetical thinking about how life might be lived, but there has been little application of what is read to experience.[48]

Franciscus agrees with Augustinus's analysis of the problem but not with the solution. Augustinus proposes a return to the meditative practices of the past. Franciscus prefers those of the present: he is convinced that his lyric poetry is a valid form of reflective activity and a new type of ethically oriented contemplative practice. But he adds an important caveat: this engagement produces the desired result only if his poems are read properly, that is, if they are read like the meditative texts of the ancients, both pagan and Christian. What he is suggesting is ethical praxis based on poetry—an unacceptable position from the viewpoint of Plato and Augustine but not, let us note, from the perspective of Dante, who is Petrarch's predecessor in the use of this technique, although in a different manner, in the ethereal verse of the *Paradiso*. This part of the *Commedia* leads the reader upward from the sensory engagements of the *Inferno* and *Purgatorio* toward an appreciation of the divine, which no words can adequately describe.

In short, the message of the *Secretum* is directed at us, as Petrarch's readers, and what it tells us is how to read his poetry—meditatively, as it was composed: to reflect on the meaning of the individual lyrics in the collection rather than being dazzled by the verbal effects alone. For Petrarch is convinced, as Coleridge later proposes, that poetry is a kind of philosophy. No less than Plato or Augustine, he has embarked on a spiritual journey in quest of self-knowledge. As his readers, we follow his "wanderings," in which the events of a story, as they are recorded in the *Confessions*, have been replaced by sudden, unpredictable changes in emotional states, leading, as Gur Zak has proposed, in a circular rather than a linear direction, which has endless, attractive pathways but no final destination.[49] This is not religious meditation, which is what Augustinus has in mind, somewhat anachronistically reflecting the practices of fourteenth-century spiritual thinkers: it is a return to the meditative practices of the ancient world, which are now redeployed in order to gain insights into the self via another secular pursuit, namely lyric poetry.

There is one well-known objection to this sort of interpretation of Petrarch's endeavor. This concerns his self-confident conception of himself as an author. Augustinus argues that this is certain evidence of pride. But Petrarch has a subtle answer, even if it is not entirely convincing. He believes that contemplative practices that he associates with writing and reading justify his activity as an author. He does not deny that he desires to achieve immortality through his writings. But the Horatian dictum is combined with the notion that authorship is morally justified, provided that the configuration that the author presents of himself in his works is recognized by him and his audience to be a literary fiction. This portrait of the author can then be viewed as one transient image among others and, as such, separated from the permanent values that are acquired through meditation on the classics and the Bible. In the *Secretum*'s preface Petrarch recommends that his *libellus* should be mulled over by readers, who are presumably in search of truth, as are the characters in the debate.

Petrarch's views on the ethics of reading and writing are explored differently in the *Canzoniere*, which was written between 1342 and 1371. It is here rather than in the *Secretum* that we find his equivalent of the spiritual autobiography of the *Confessions*. Augustine asks how a life story, experienced in fragments, can be unified and given permanent meaning through meditation on Christ; in the *Canzoniere*

Petrarch asks whether such permanence can be generated and sustained by means of poetic images alone. He also inquires whether this can be done without the intervention of a third party, that is, a spiritual guide who leads the reader upward, as Vergil guides Dante through the *Inferno* and *Purgatorio*. He transforms Dante's approach to poetry as a vehicle for reflections on the self as well as Augustine's notion that the central text for analysis in this setting is the author's narrative life history.[50] He does not discuss himself within an exegetical framework, as does Dante in the *Vita Nuova*, nor against the backdrop of larger historical events, as in the *Commedia*. And while he renews Augustine's practice of the soliloquy, he reworks this form into a dialogue with himself and his readers by means of poetry.

The only guide we have to self-analysis in the *Canzoniere* is reading itself. Petrarch asks his readers to consider how words, as they create conflicting responses in the self-conscious subject, can, at the same time as they are experienced, be held in the mind along with the knowledge of their present temporariness and their absent permanence. He would like to achieve this equilibrium, as writer and reader, but he is not sure that he is capable of doing so. As a consequence, his dilemma is more profound than that of Augustine.

The impasse is represented in the *Secretum* through Franciscus's inability to explain to Augustinus why poetry is important, and by Augustinus's inability to convince Franciscus of the opposite view. There is no solution for Petrarch beyond the sustaining of an ethical outlook by means of the reader's will. This is an Augustinian solution, but in the *Confessions* the reader attempts to adjust his or her interpretation of what is taking place to the will of God, whereas in Petrarch there is no omniscient presence to which he can attach his fleeting impressions of his relationship with Laura. It is possible to conclude that there can be none for the reader either. But Petrarch does not take this step in the *Secretum* or the *Canzoniere*: he limits himself to pointing out the potential role of poetry in shaping the individual's ethical outlook, in contrast to the restatement of Plato's view in the autobiography of his mentor.

For Augustine, let us recall, there is only one true book, namely scripture: only one Word, into which all human words somehow fit.[51] For Dante there are two interdependent books, namely scripture, as an ideal literary structure, and the "the book of memory," which is a human invention, subject to recall. In both books the pages recording individual lives are scattered in Plotinian fashion throughout the world, resulting in multiplicity rather than unity of perspective. By contrast in Petrarch the reader is in possession of the pages alone, which are symbolized by the 366 lyrics that comprise the *Canzoniere*. There is no "book" that unifies those leaves into a single volume, as there is in different senses for Augustine and Dante: a literary form that, through ascetic reading, permits the individual to integrate the fragments of his or her life into a whole. For Petrarch, the relevant "book" can exist only as a putative and intentional structure: it is a desire, wish, or unverified statement about the future, rather than an article of faith. He attempts to overcome his sense of textual dispersal in his letters by conversing with great figures from the past, such as Cicero, in order to provide a continuity for his thinking, but the presence of these authors only serves to emphasize the distance separating the *antiqui* and *moderni*.

In Petrarch, therefore, the phenomenological appreciation of time induced by the Augustinian *distentio animi* is both a psychological and a historical experience. Transferred to the realm of lyric poetry, this view accounts for his sense of permanence within fragility, as, for example, in the opening two stanzas of poem 17, in which, Rosanna Bettarini remarks, there is a "scission" between the speaking "I," which recalls the personal, individual, and subjective first-person of the troubadour poets, writing in the "new sweet style," and the more profound "I" of the Augustinian-Platonic tradition, in which the present is invaded by the past and looks forward in hope to a higher form of sapiential vision:[52]

> Piovonmi amare lagrime dal viso
> con un vento angoscioso di sospiri,
> quando in voi adiven che gli occhi giri
> per cui sola dal mondo i' son diviso.
>
> Vero è che 'l dolce mansüeto riso
> per acqueta gli ardenti miei desiri,
> et mi sottragge al foco de' martiri,
> mentr'io son a mirarvi intento et fiso. . . .
>
> [What bitter tears fall raining from my face
> Whenever, with an anguished storm of sighs,
> It happens that I turn my eyes on you
> By whom, alone, I'm cut off from the world.
>
> Your sweet and gentle laughter, it is true,
> At last abates the flames of my desire
> And from the martyr's fire delivers me
> While earnestly on you I fix my gaze]. . . .

Petrarch's appreciation of the combined ascetic and aesthetic dimensions of reading was transferred to numerous authors in the following three centuries by means of the imitation or emulation of the style of the *Canzoniere*, known as "Petrarchism." An important role in spreading this view was played by the humanist and cardinal Pietro Bembo, whose treatise *Prose della volgar lingua*, published in 1525,

33

legitimized the use of the vernacular, as contrasted with Latin, as an appropriate vehicle for Italian poetic discourse, and chose Petrarch's lyrics as the model for that discourse.

By uniting classical Latin, Provençal, and Sicilian poetry, as well as the *dolce stil nuovo* and the innovations of Dante, Petrarch was judged to have struck a balance between ancient and modern. The *aesthetic* deployment of the style, meters, and vocabulary of the *Canzoniere* conferred an *ascetic* legitimacy to such verse forms as the sonnet, madrigal, ballad, sestina, and canzone, thus making fidelity to Petrarch's poetic genres a component in establishing ethical legitimacy for all Renaissance poetry. In his treatise on love, *Gli Asolani*, written in 1505, Bembo utilized Petrarch, as Petrarch had utilized Augustine, as a source of Neoplatonic thinking about love. Through the imitation of his verse forms by such poets as Giovanni della Casa, Thomas Wyatt, Pierre de Ronsard, and Juan Boscán, Petrarch became the first European poet to influence a number of different national literatures by means of vernacular poetry. To illustrate the transfer of the Petarachan metaphor of reading to such poetry, it suffices to quote a few lines from the first sonnet in Sir Philip Sidney's *Astrophel and Stella* (1581–1582):

> Loving in truth, and fain in verse my love to show,
> That she, dear she, might take some pleasure of my
>   pain,
> Pleasure might cause her read, reading might make her
>   know,
> Knowledge might pity win, and pity grace obtain,
> I sought fit words to paint the blackest face of woe:
> Studying inventions fine, her wits to entertain,
> Oft turning others' leaves, to see if thence would flow
> Some fresh and fruitful showers upon my sunburn'd
>   brain.[53]

The Reader's Dilemma

The contribution of Montaigne to the ethics of reading, to which I now turn, was linked to Petrarchism in a number of ways. Like the *Canzoniere*, the *Essais* consist in a loosely organized group of spiritual exercises in which the author, employing the prose essay rather than the lyric poem, sets out in search of stability and self-understanding. No less than Petrarch's poems, letters, and *Secretum*, the *Essais* transform the art of conversational dialogue.[54] They do not develop their themes logically; and, if there is a "philosophy," Michael Screech observes, it is, like Petrarch's, wise and practical, always progressing but never finished, and all times frank and personal.[55] Both authors are concerned with reading as a metaphor for self-exploration: the preface to the *Secretum*, where Truth, representing the reader, sits in judgment on Petrarch, is a good introduction to Montaigne's *Essais*. The poet, no less than the essayist, can say that he is the only true subject of his book.

Along with Plato, Aristotle, Plutarch, and Cicero, Augustine is one of Montaigne's philosophical counselors on the use of reading in the search for the contemplative life.[56] Augustine and Montaigne stand at either end of a lengthy historical development in which reading and asceticism influence each other. Augustine codifies thinking on the subject in late antiquity, while Montaigne does so near the end of the Renaissance. But their perspectives differ, and this difference has a good deal to do with the problematizing of relations between reading and ethics previously outlined by Petrarch and other secular poets during the early Renaissance.

Put succinctly, in Augustine the sifting of ancient methods of self-inquiry results in the emergence of a single synthetic form, which is represented by the confessional autobiography, just as the theological adventures of his youth end in his reaffirmation of confidence in a monotheistic faith. In Montaigne, there is a comparable sorting out of positions and a search for answers, but there is no satisfactory conclusion to the inquiry at either a literary or a personal level. His questioning simply continues throughout the *Essais*, moving aporetically from one topic to another. This is a fitting conclusion to a type of conversation that begins in Plato's early dialogues, in which Socrates' debates with his pupils frequently complement soliloquies within himself—questions and answers on ethical problems for which there is no final solution.[57] Centuries later, Augustine, employing a similar method, learns a great deal from his studies, above all, as noted, "how to read."[58] The results of this lesson are evident in the intellectual progress represented by books 1 to 8 of the *Confessions*. By contrast, Montaigne is amused and taught much through his reading, but he does not acquire a method he is certain will lead him to a sensible and humane philosophy of life.

In Augustine, the quest inspired by a reading culture reaches its goal, which is the personal certainty of faith. In Petrarch, the goal is always in sight, even if it is never reached. However, in Montaigne journey and destination are indistinguishable. As a result the very notion of a final objective for the reading process is questioned. In the *Essais*, the venerable ascetic model of reading envisaged in book 1, which is based on the analysis of the content of ancient writings, is little by little whittled away, until by book 3 it is less credible than the acceptance of experience as a foundation for ethical judgments. Accompanying this perspective, there is a change in emphasis from reading as a source of information to the psychological dimensions of reading and writing. Montaigne is as interested in what his books contain as he is in what they do to him. This is a new and troubling ascetic quest, for which answers will later be sought in psychology rather than in literature.

This attitude began to take shape early in his career, when, isolated in his château in southwest France, he acquired the means to lead a life of erudite leisure but, once established on his domaine, succeeded only in falling into melancholy. It was the writing of his *Essais*, rather than the conclusions he reached in his inquiries, that stabilized his personality and permitted him to control his negative thinking.[59] In this respect he presents an example of the transition between the medieval and the early modern outlook on contemplative disciplines, which dates from the fourteenth century, well illustrated, among others, by Petrarch. This consists in the substitution or complementing of the habit of reading with ascetic writing: the use of writing as a therapeutic tool for calming the passions, exteriorizing anxieties, and realizing an intentional design for life.

This dimension of the *Essais* is evident from their strategy of organization.[60] Their genesis consists in a simple spiritual exercise, namely Montaigne's habit of soliloquizing. He listens to himself as he speaks silently within his mind; in this oral discourse he goes over alternatives of thought and action that are based on either his reading or his observations.[61] These mental exercises, which take place before any words are written, are not rediscoverable through his published texts, although clues to his manner of proceeding are given in his variants, glosses, and centos.[62] Proceeding within, soliloquies permit Montaigne to detach himself from extraneous influences and to concentrate on the phenomena of his own consciousness. He wants to move from reading to a textless presence, in which he can presumably see himself as he is. His writing is a means of self-expression as well as an example of risk taking, as Thomas Greene has observed: a constant struggle between the internal and the external that is brought about by his method of composition.[63]

His goal is at once literary, ethical,[64] and meditative, as is evident from the construction of the *Essais*. The successive "chapters" are not published in modern editions in the order in which they were written; on the contrary, each segment of an essay may contain sentences and phrases that were written at different times. Also, the parts were not initially divided into paragraphs; that too is the work of modern editors. Montaigne evidently intended his readers to pick up his book and to put it down, just as he jotted down thoughts as they came to him. The method is associative, not sequential, and the associations include both the products of his imagination as well as the images generated by his reading of the Latin poets. He is a member of no school: he draws on Stoic, Skeptic, and Epicurean thinking as he wishes. Because they are meditations, the chronology of these thoughts is unimportant: what interests him is a feature of their nontemporality, namely the way in which, within each essay, his reflections return by different routes to the same theme: a method that involves repetition and variations rather than logical order. Like Petrarch, who constantly revised the ordering of his letters and poems, Montaigne was continually adding words and phrases to what he had written: examples, quotations, and arguments in a cumulative rather than rational manner. The complexity is increased by the fact that he was frequently thinking in Latin while writing in French.

Montaigne does not claim, as does Descartes a generation later, that book learning has taught him nothing certain and that as a consequence he must begin his quest for indubitable knowledge again, using only reason.[65] He nonetheless finishes one age of reflection on the value of the reading process and begins another. He concludes the long period that encompasses late antiquity, the Middle Ages, and the Renaissance, in which different arguments are pursued for the justification of reading as an aid to moral and ethical thinking. He inaugurates the modern age, in which it is assumed that reading, like other arts of language and rhetoric, is too unreliable a mode of communication to provide a foundation for certain judgments on ethical matters or, for that matter, on anything else. Theories of reading since Montaigne further restrict the field of interpretation by deploying Montaigne's method, that is, by applying the doctrines of ancient Skepticism to literary criticism.[66] Montaigne is the starting point for challenging the ancient and medieval belief in the ability of reading to set up common lines of communication between individual minds, proposing on the contrary that minds remains isolated, unknowable, and, despite the efforts of language, unable to communicate on central issues in ethics.

4

I conclude with an example of this type of dissociation that is found in another scene of reading: in chapters 11 and 19 of part 1, "The Window," in Virginia Woolf's novel *To the Lighthouse*, published in 1927.

The problem of reading and other minds is introduced in *To the Lighthouse* in chapter 19 (of part 1). At this point in the novel Mrs. Ramsay has entered the room in the family's rented summerhouse on an island in the Hebrides in which her husband is seated reading a book. The scene follows a splendid dinner party (chapter 17) to which all their vacation guests have been invited. During the feast a number of conjectures are made concerning the reputations of once popular nineteenth-century poets and novelists.

After dinner Mr. Ramsay withdraws to another room. We next see him through the eyes of his wife as he betrays exterior signs of the interior enjoyment arising from what is clearly the aesthetic rereading of a text that has given him pleasure at some moment in the distant past. Unlike other examples of the "stream of consciousness" technique in the novel, which are concerned with the direct impression that the characters are making on Mrs. Ramsay, this passage utilizes the intermediary of the reading process to create a putative connection between her thoughts and those of her husband:

> She looked at her husband (taking up her stocking and beginning to knit), and saw that he did not wish to be interrupted—that was clear. He was reading something that moved him very much. He was half smiling and then she knew he was controlling his emotion. He was tossing the pages over. He was acting it—perhaps he was thinking himself the person in the book. She wondered what book it was. Oh, it was one of old Sir Walter's. . . .[67]

This, of course, is mind reading, not the reading of a text, but it is based on the observation of another person who is reviewing in his mind a text that he has read and, perhaps unaware that he is being observed, expresses his appreciation in a manner that is visible to others. The romances of Sir Walter Scott, which he is leafing through, were the most popular books in England during the nineteenth century.[68] Over dinner, in the novel's previous scene, Charles Tansley, who is notorious for his dissenting views on many subjects, "denounced" Scott's Waverley Novels, even though it was evident to others at the party that he had not read them thoroughly. His remarks have to be seen in context: he was responding to the uncritical praise of Scott by another guest, the elderly botanist William Bankes, and to the warm but unvoiced approval of Mrs. Ramsay herself.

The question that chapter 19 asks is why Mr. Ramsay has buried himself in one of Scott's novels after the entertainments that accompanied this sumptuous dinner. According to the author, who makes a rare intervention at this point, it is because he thinks that in time people will not read his books, just as they do not any longer read those of Scott. We hear this conclusion in Mrs. Ramsay's internal voice, as she relates her husband's thoughts:

"That's what they'll say of me"; so he went and got one of those books [i.e., one of Scott's books]. And if he came to the conclusion, "That's true," what Charles Tansley said, he would accept it about Scott. (She could see that he was weighing, considering, putting this with that as he read). But not about himself. That troubled her. He would always be worrying about his own books—will they be read, are they good, why aren't they better, what do people think of me?

A second text now enters the scene. Mrs. Ramsay, as she knits, repeats in her head, silently, some verses that her husband had recited during dinner. The couple sit together in the study, wordlessly mulling over passages of verse or prose that each has read before, while their thoughts take them elsewhere: in Mr. Ramsay's, into fantasies about himself; in Mrs. Ramsay's, into meditation on her husband's insecurities and the reasons for their mutual isolation from each other over the long years of their marriage. These are working examples of a venerable technique, *lectio spiritualis*. And, in an unobtrusive way, Virginia Woolf has introduced into the topos of the "scene of reading" an element that is old as Abelard and Dante, namely unfulfilled love.

The Ramsays observe each other as they sit alone, while the other guests clear the dishes, chatter with each other, or return to their personal interests. As the pair look at each other, physically close but mentally apart, the reader becomes aware that the texts they are musing over are symbols of a problem in communication that lies at the center of the novel's action: this concerns the degree that one person can ever know another, and the capacity of individuals for assuming that the language of their thoughts accurately mirrors the "languages" of the world in which they live. It is a problem that was being talked about by Moore, Russell, and above all by Wittgenstein in the years just before *To the Lighthouse* was published.[69]

As the scene unfolds, the aesthetic enjoyment of the texts gives way to an ascetic orientation—the sense in Mrs. Ramsay that the act of reading can create mental spaces that draw attention to individuals' mutual isolation. Therefore, one of the purposes of reading is ascetic, namely trying to overcome the feeling of alienation to which reading itself has given rise. In taking up this topic Virginia Woolf employs a technique for which her novels are often remarked: the awareness in her characters of "a sharp contrast . . . between the brief span of time occupied by the exterior event and the dreamlike wealth of a process of consciousness which traverses a whole subjective universe . . .": a process in which "the exterior events have actually lost their hegemony" and instead "serve to release and interpret interior events."[70] In chapter 19, the vehicle for this experience is a scene of reading. In contrast to those of Abelard and Dante, it is one in which the man reads for emotional satisfaction, while the woman seeks and finds a pathway to inner reflective experience. It is a feminist's view of meditative ascent, not the first in the subject's literature but one of the most powerful in the novel's history.

What is the source of this ascetic impulse? A clue to the

author's thinking on the subject is found in chapter 19, although it is carefully hidden from view. This concerns her introduction of the classic stages in the meditative process into Mrs. Ramsay's reflections. In proceeding from chapters 17 to 19 the reader has already covered the first stage, namely the passage from the senses to the mind. The feast is narrated in highly sensuous language. As E. M. Forster reminds us, "the great dish of Boeuf en Daube which forms the centre of the dinner of union . . ." is the element in the novel "around which all that section of the book coheres. . . ."[71] Once the meal has finished, we find ourselves in an interior, psychological type of writing, from which the vivid descriptions of chapter 17 are absent.

A second stage of the meditative process then takes place. We observe that Mrs. Ramsay is knitting all the while she is observing her husband lost in thought, as he flips over the pages of one of Scott's novels. Knitting frequently precedes Mrs. Ramsay's inner thoughts, which are subsequently conveyed to the reader through the interplay of consciousness itself. The sensations of chapter 17, then, are not ends in themselves: they are superseded, as the mind moves inward and upward, by the equally vivid portrayal of nonsensory events. Virginia Woolf, like her predecessors, is concerned with the inner and outer lives of two individuals, and the degree to which life's anxieties arise from the awareness of a disjunction between them. The novel's title makes subtle use of the traditional symbol of light in order to demonstrate the unrealized potential of mortals for this sort of illumination. The postponed journey represents the difficulties that individuals like Mr. Ramsay place before themselves, which make it impossible for them to reach this goal. In the unmetaphysical universe of Virginia Woolf only this sort of quest for self-knowledge is permitted.

The passage in which this aspect of Virginia Woolf's outlook is most clearly revealed is found in chapter 11 (of part 1). We enter this scene, which prepares the way for chapter 19, at the moment when Mrs. Ramsay has finished her domestic duties and put her children to bed. She finds herself with the luxury of a little time to herself:

For now she need not think about anybody. She could be herself, by herself. And that was what now she often felt the need of—to think; well not even to think. To be silent; to be alone. All the being and the doing, expansive, glittering, vocal, evaporated; and one shrunk, with a sense of solemnity, to being oneself, a wedge-shaped core of darkness, something invisible to others.

If later we will pass from the senses to the mind and from unfocused to focused attention, this preparatory passage illustrates another pair of themes traditionally associated with meditation, namely silence and solitude. In this wordless, interior universe, which Mrs. Ramsay discovers in rare moments of relaxation in the evening, she is able to isolate the various elements in the "stream of consciousness" and to follow their passage through the mind: to pick them up or drop them at will, and to unite them with other impressions by means of memory. She continues:

When life sank down for a moment, the range of experience seemed limitless. And to everybody there was always this sense of unlimited resources, she supposed. . . . Beneath it is all dark, it is all spreading, it is unfathomably deep; but now and again we rise to the surface and that is what you see us by. Her horizon seemed to her limitless. . . . There was freedom, there was peace, there was, most welcome of all, a summoning together, a resting on a platform of stability.

Finally, there is a still higher phase of this type of contemplation, more common in Eastern than in Western accounts of meditation, in which Mrs. Ramsay recognizes the necessity of doing away with one's self altogether in order to enjoy briefly an experience of pure being:

Not as oneself did one find rest ever, in her experience (she accomplished here something dexterous with her needles), but as a wedge of darkness. Losing personality, one lost the fret, the hurry, the stir; and there rose to her lips always some exclamation of triumph over life when things came together in this peace, this rest, this eternity; and pausing there she looked out to meet that stroke of the lighthouse, the long steady stroke, the last of the three, which was her stroke. . . . Often she found herself sitting and looking, sitting and looking, with her work in her hands until she became the thing she looked at—that light for example.

The passage ends with another repetition, this time in words, which recalls the situation in which the chapter opens, namely the pictures of the refrigerator and mowing machine that her son, James, has cut out of a newspaper. Mrs. Ramsay begins chapter 11 by telling herself that "children never forget," and what James will never forget is his father's thoughtless remark, with which the novel opens, to the effect that the weather will not permit them to go by water to visit the nearby lighthouse on the following day. No, Mrs. Ramsay says to herself,

"Children don't forget, children don't forget"—which she would repeat and begin adding to it, It will end, It will end, she said. It will come, it will come, when suddenly she added, We are in the hands of the Lord.

This eschatological dimension is immediately refused in the traditional language in which it has been brought forward but then rehabilitated in other terms:

But instantly she was annoyed with herself for saying that. Who had said it? not she; she had been trapped into saying something she did not mean. She looked up over her knitting and met the third stroke and it seemed to her like her own eyes meeting her own eyes, searching as she alone could search into her mind and her heart, purifying out of existence that lie, any lie. She praised herself in praising that light, without vanity, for she was stern, she was searching, she was beautiful like that light.

The Christian form of meditation, which may have been in the background of her thinking, is replaced by the Romantic, which culminates in the contemplation of nature:

It was odd, she thought, how if one was alone, one leant to things, inanimate things: trees, streams, flowers; felt they expressed one; felt they became one; felt they knew one; in a sense were one; felt an irrational tenderness thus (she looked at the long steady light) as for oneself. There rose, and she looked and looked with her needles suspended, there curled up off the roof of the mind, rose from the lake of one's being, a mist, a bride to meet her lover.

"Bride" and "lover" take us back to the *Song of Songs*, one of the points of departure for Western mystical thought. The last phase of Mrs. Ramsay's secular ascent likewise echoes the traditional themes of light, silence, grace, and love, as described by Augustine, Dante, and others. And finally there are "three strokes"—a trinity, the last of which is hers, the holy spirit: for it is she who leaves the others in a final stage of meditative progress, as she is transformed from a symbol of consciousness to one of transcendence.

2   The Ascetic Reader

My discussion so far has focused on a dilemma that arose from two attitudes toward literary experience that took shape in the ancient world, namely reading for pleasure and reading for moral improvement. These attitudes have had an important relationship with each other over the centuries since the distinction was given canonical expression by Plato and Augustine.

As an example of this interdependence, I analyzed a literary topos that I call the "scene of reading" as it is presented in Abelard, Dante, and Virginia Woolf. I also commented briefly on the manner in which some problems in ethics and literature are dealt with by Petrarch and Montaigne. In the following two lectures I would like to examine these issues as they arise in independent traditions of ascetic and aesthetic readership.

This lecture is concerned with ascetic reading and tackles the subject within three successive periods of history: (1) late antiquity, when asceticism is given a significant role in Christianity; (2) the Middle Ages, when reading becomes a major means of organizing ascetic practices; and (3) the early modern period, when secular forms of asceticism re-emerge in the West.

.   .   .

I begin with some introductory remarks on the history of asceticism, out of which the notion of an "ascetic reader" arises. The terms are derived from the Greek word *askēsis*, which originally meant exercise or training and was later associated with the discipline necessary for living a variety of rule-bound, ethically oriented lifestyles.

Many ancient philosophies and all traditional religions have a commitment to some form of asceticism. This involves such activities as fasting, seclusion, sexual constraint, physical austerities, mental restrictions, as well as renunciation of material goods and worldly attachments.

A distinction can be made between the non-moral advocacy of such practices, which have as their goal ritual purity or cleanliness, and morally oriented asceticism, in which programs of self-denial are viewed as a step toward inner or spiritual betterment. It is in this form that asceticism is found in classical Jainism, Tibetan Buddhism, Judaism, and Christianity.

Another distinction, admittedly less precise, can be made between ascetical routines in nonliterate and literate religions. Among nonliterates asceticism is compulsory for all members of the community through such practices as puberty rites, initiation ceremonies, and dietary laws, which are widespread in tribal, nomadic, or agrarian societies. Among literate religions, whether polytheistic or monotheistic, asceticism is normally voluntary. Freedom of choice is both a prerequisite of asceticism and the framework within which believers situate its ethical significance. In literate religions, such practices usually form part of an articulated theology and involve written regulations, as in the Sufi movement in Islam or monasticism in Christianity.

Nineteenth-century commentators on asceticism were chiefly concerned with its internal dimension. Arthur Schopenhauer, who is discussed in the next lecture, speaks of asceticism in a "narrow sense" as "the intentional breaking of the will by the refusal of what is agreeable and the selection of what is disagreeable: the voluntarily chosen life of penance and self-chastisement for the continual mortification of the will."[1] This approach to asceticism, echoed by Ernst Trocltsch, has an Augustinian and Lutherian flavor, inasmuch as attention is directed to a combination of interiority and intentionality. In this context asceticism may be said to refer to voluntary, reiterated, and organized procedures that promote internal self-discipline, as well as to the emotional and cognitive accompaniments of those procedures.

Important contributions to the notion of inner asceticism were made by Max Weber (d. 1920), who studied the connections between the ethical and social aspects of different religions. Weber divided ascetic practices into two types, world rejecting and world embracing (*weltablehnende und innerweltliche Askese*).[2] The first involves total withdrawal from the world, "from social and psychological ties with the family, from the possession of worldly goods and from political, economic, and erotic activities." Here, participation in the world is looked upon as approval of the world, and leads invariably to alienation from God. By contrast, innerworldly asceticism requires the individual to participate in the world in order to achieve salvation: "more precisely, [to work] within the institutions of the world but in opposition to them." In this case the world is the individual's responsibility, and, as fulfillment of ascetic obligations, he (or she) may feel obliged to improve, transform, or radically change the world. In this perspective asceticism, and even ascetic readership, can be part of a program that has social as well as intellectual goals.

Weber applied his thinking on asceticism chiefly to the activity of Protestant sects during the rise of capitalism— a topic that has given rise to a large historical debate on the "work ethic."[3] Also, in order to sharpen the contrast between this-worldly and otherworldly "ideal types," he introduced into his writings the controversial distinction between asceticism and mysticism. On this view, the Christian ascetic is characterized by activity in the world, and this activity assists him or her in attaining his ultimate goal, namely the realization of God's grace. The individual's assurance arises from the certitude of the promise of salvation and from the personal knowledge that through his actions he serves his maker. His opposition to the world is not a flight from the world but a series of willed victories over temptations. He is obliged to combat these allurements again and again, even though he has no guarantee that definitive victory can be won over them and as a consequence over himself. By contrast, the mystic has as his goal not activity, however defined, but contemplation. He desires to achieve repose in God and in him alone. His orientation is away from the world and toward what appears externally to be a kind of leisured inactivity. By following the path of increasing self-awareness, the mystic attempts to achieve a perception of overall meaning for the world—a sense of oneness with all things and with God. Once this insight is attained, he may engage in practical activities in the world. But these are not the initial objective.

One of Weber's insights was to have noted that the contrast between ascetical and mystical types of behavior is clearest when the implications of rejecting the world are not yet completely realized. The ascetic, in acting in an inner-worldly fashion, is obliged to close his or her mind to the question of the world's ultimate meaning. It suffices that through rational actions in the world he or she is personally executing God's will, even though it is admitted that this will is unknowable to ordinary mortals. By contrast, the mystic is concerned with understanding the meaning of the world, which cannot be perceived rationally, since the type of unity that this meaning represents is not understandable by means of the logical methods used to establish human knowledge. In these "incomplete" scenarios fall most significant Western writings about asceticism and mysticism.

2

While ascetic practices are found in both the Old and New Testaments, they are not essential to the rites of either Judaism or Christianity. In this respect, the Western history of the subject contrasts with that of the East, where asceticism is well entrenched in Jainism, Buddhism, and Hinduism by the beginning of the Common Era.[4]

The situation changes considerably in late antiquity, when there are numerous statements on asceticism by Gnostics, Manichaeans, and pagans, the latter including Porphyry's important treatise on the merits of vegetarianism. The church fathers were aware that Pythagoras and Plato had given a role to asceticism in creating a philosophical outlook;[5] both are praised by Augustine in his early dialogue *De Ordine*.[6] Christian thinkers likewise knew that high value was placed on mental and physical training by Stoics, as illustrated by the writings of Seneca and Epictetus, as well as by Cynics, Epicureans, and Neoplatonists. As a consequence, in some pagan and Christian writings on the ethical life there is considerable overlap in the connotative fields of the terms "asceticism" and "philosophy."

Judaism was both a philosophical and nonphilosophical influence on the formation of Christian asceticism. As it appears in the writings of Philo of Alexandria, Jewish thinking on the subject is indistinct from that of pagans, since, following Aristobulus, he was convinced that Judaism was the one true philosophy, which had contributed in significant ways to the views of Plato and his successors on the nature and pursuit of the happy life. Yet, despite the importance of Philo for Alexandrian theology, attitudes toward philosophy differed considerably among the Greek and Latin fathers. Justin Martyr, Clement of Alexandria, and Gregory of Nyssa believed in the compatibility of philosophy and Christianity. Origen (d. c. 254), is more difficult to evaluate, since his major treatise, *De Principiis*, has not survived. According to Eusebius, he led an ascetical life from youth that included fasts, vigils, voluntary poverty, and even self-mutilation; however, he also attended the lectures on literature and philosophy delivered by Ammonius Saccas, the founder of Neoplatonism. Tertullian, the first significant Latin theologian (d. c. 220), was educated as a pagan, but on conversion to Christianity abandoned philosophy and became an admirer of Montanism, in which the laxness of the church's attitude toward fasting and penance is criticized.

At a practical level Christian asceticism in both East and West took a good deal of its inspiration from the Old Testament. The biblical example of voluntary poverty was a powerful antidote to Roman luxury and materialism. Ascetic discipline provided a model for moral improvement in society—a theme that is present in Plato's *Republic* and, based on reading, is reintroduced in Thomas More's *Utopia*, discussed below. The Jewish practice of living according to rules, despite Paul's accusation of "legalism," fortified the

tenuous beliefs of many early Christians against compet-
ing religious doctrines, some of which promised spiritual
advancement without great personal sacrifice, for example
Neoplatonism and Gnosticism. Through the reinterpreta-
tion of ritual occasions that were Jewish in origin, such as
Passover, early Christianity began to see itself as a religion
fundamentally different from Judaism.[7]

Pachomius (d. 346) was the first to gather Christian ascetic principles together and to organize them as a "rule" for
governing religious communities on such matters as work,
prayer, food, clothing, and living conditions. By the fourth
century ascetics following such regulations were found in
several regions of the Middle East: Egypt, Palestine, Syria,
Mesopotamia, Armenia, Pontus, and Cappadocia, as well
as in Western Gaul, owing to the missionary activities of
St. Martin (d. 400). As asceticism took shape in these locali-
ties it was notable for its innovative attitude toward children and women. Although monastic houses usually contained adults, they early accepted children as young as six
to seven years old. As a consequence, ascetic practices were
not confined to those who had undergone a long initiation,
as in many philosophical schools, but were open to recruits
in earlier stages of life. Also, Christian asceticism was notable in its accessibility to women, who frequently exceeded
men in their devotion to self-denial.[8] This was the earliest
form of a specifically female spirituality in Western religious history, for which there is no precedent in the ancient
world.

In the *Historia Lausiaca*, Palladius (d. 425) eloquently
relates the life histories of some seventy notable ascetics.
Other contemporary accounts of the phenomenon include
the *Historia Monachorum*, the anonymous *Apophthegmata*,
or Sayings of the Fathers, the *Religious History* of Theodo-

ret, bishop of Cyrrhus, and Athanasius's *Vita Antonii*. The last-mentioned work was translated into Latin by Evagrius of Antioch (d. 399) and influenced both Ambrose's and Augustine's conception of the monastic life, as well as that of numerous medieval authors, including Francis of Assisi. The ascetic themes presented in early histories of the Christian life were popularized through the *Collationes* of John Cassian (d. 435), which record conversations with some twenty-four figures residing in desert communities, many of which the author visited.

These "conferences" represent an important milestone in the synthesis of Western ascetic doctrines. They are individualistic in tone, each monk speaking for himself, but share a commitment to an activist biblical theology, which is frequently presented in terms that seem to complement the ancient philosophical pursuit of virtue. The solitary religious life is compared to soldiering or farming: the dangers or labors are cheerfully endured,[9] in view, so to speak, of peace after battle or abundant harvests. Prayer and meditation provide an occasion for spiritual reminiscence (*spiritalis memoriae . . . occasio*), in which thoughts, freed from mundane associations, ascend toward a lost and rediscovered paradise.[10] Lacking these stabilizing forces, the soul is continuously in motion,[11] tossed to and fro, owing to inertia or imprudence (*desidia uel imprudentia*). Such wanderings (*euagationes*) can be brought to an end only through a sustained effort of body and mind.[12] The workshop in which the necessary skills are acquired is the mental cell,[13] where the battle to master the soul's disequilibrium is won by discipline and determination.[14]

Bodily and spiritual exercises are not sources of perfection in themselves but instruments for achieving perfection (*non perfectio sed perfectionis instrumenta*). They are the tools of the ascetic's trade, just as a knowledge of public speaking is utilized by the trained orator.[15] The goal is the purification of the heart and the overcoming of its innate fragility. Former lives are abandoned, and souls are unburdened of the debris left behind by spent passions.[16] In coping with earlier experience,[17] prayer and interior discipline are like way stations on a lengthy, arduous journey, which takes place in both life and mind. Reading plays a prominent role in this transition (whether one reads for oneself or listens to others reading).[18] Renunciation is first corporeal, then emotional and spiritual, thus surmounting all visible, tangible, and physical things as the gaze moves upward beyond the self.[19]

The devotion to ascetic practices revealed in accounts of the desert fathers is anticipated by the little that is known about the Essenes and Therapeutae. The latter were Jewish sectarian communities active from the second century B.C.E., which are described and interpreted by Philo of Alexandria. In his youthful treatise *Quod Omnis Probus Liber Sit*, Philo declares that the Essenes are not interested in logic or science but in ethics, on which they hold weekly discussions in which passages of scripture are read aloud by one member of the community and explained morally and allegorically by another.[20] Flavius Joseph and Pliny confirm the use of reading in prayer, silent meditation, and rites of purification, while Philo's description of the Therapeutae, in *De Vita Contemplativa*, provides details concerning the use of reading as therapy for the soul and as a means of achieving a contemplative state of mind. Food and drink are excluded from Therapeutae sanctuaries; the law, prophets, and psalms are read, commented upon, and utilized in liturgy. The members of the community meditate on scripture while awake or asleep, live in silence six days of the week, and believe that self-control is the chief source of virtue.[21]

Like their Jewish predecessors (with whom they apparently had no historical connection), the desert fathers behave bookishly while at the same time they are distressed by unnecessary displays of book learning. They are uneasy with worldly education, in which rhetorical, instrumental, or commercial types of reading take precedence over spirituality. Many stories about reading in early monastic histories camouflage the institutions of higher learning or replace them with a combination of local orality and the supernatural. In Palladius's *Lives of the Desert Fathers*, for example, written around 420, the monk Didymus is said to be blind from the age of four; he was allegedly instructed in reading, interpretation, and foretelling the future by his "conscience." Yet elsewhere we discover that Didymus learned to read by means of raised letters on the page—possibly the earliest account of reading by touch.[22] Abba Or, who was said to be illiterate, nonetheless knew how to read and interpret scripture when he arrived from the desert in Alexandria.[23] Theon, another migrant, received "heavenly instruction" in no fewer than three languages, Greek, Latin, and Egyptian.[24] The *Lives* are rich in such cautionary tales, since the Gospels, on which they are based, normally teach by means of word and example rather than through precepts or principles. When these early ascetics make use of the skills of rhetoric and logic, it is usually to combat the false confidence that classical humanistic education can inspire, as in the anecdote of St. Antony's confutation of the philosophers.[25] Skill in interpretation is the result of long years of experience and apprenticeship, requiring humility, patience, and spiritual direction.

Comparable objectives are revealed in Eastern accounts

of reading, for example in the Coptic *Life of Abbi*, which states that after the office the saint would habitually

> sit in the great common chapel . . . with his book on his knees, while even the book . . . was covered. He would open the book and gaze at it, and at once his tears would burst forth. . . . And he would not turn over a leaf, but generally had the book open at the beatitudes, or the parable of the virgins, or that of the talents. . . .[26]

Philoxenus of Mabbug (d. c. 523) writes to a brother, advising him at the third hour of the monastic day, to

> go and stand before the cross and gather your thoughts from the content of what you have read, and kneel down and implore our Lord amid tears and pain to give you the key to the meaning of the psalm. . . . See . . . that your intellect, when you perform your devotions, clearly and distinctly celebrates the contents of the psalm, and the mouth audibly. For the hymn perceptible to the senses is empty without the one conceivable by the mind. For in the same way that the body is the prerequisite for the soul and is prior to . . . consciousness, . . . the emotional song is the prerequisite for the studied hymn.

After performing the office the brother is told

> to take a book of the Fathers and read in it till the office of midday without allowing your mind to rest from the contemplation of the intellectual sentences. For do not give your external tongue an opportunity of getting, with regard to its reading, in advance of the reading of the mental tongue, but arrange the two of them so that they may run together.[27]

Despite the vividness of such accounts, statements on the topic of ascetic reading from the lives of holy persons are typically brief, isolated, and occasional, rather than forming parts of an articulated system of instruction for those entering religious communities. For more informative discussions of relations between asceticism, reading, and ethics it is necessary to turn to the writings of figures working within better-defined traditions of erudition; among these are Seneca and Augustine, who provide accounts of the functions of reading respectively in Stoicism and Christianity.

Most of Seneca's statements on the subject are found in the *Moral Epistles to Lucilius,* which were written toward the end of his life between c.e. 63 and 65.[28] Lucilius is advised not to read many books but to limit himself to works of genuine importance in shaping his philosophical outlook. From these volumes he should select maxims for memorization to be repeated to himself throughout the day. Seneca's goal is to make his student self-sufficient and to ground this autonomy on precepts working from within. In his outer life Lucilius is to follow the routines of the civil service, in which he holds a responsible position; he is to undergo no form of physical privation and to wear no garments that would set him apart from others. Within this program texts have two functions, namely reading itself and postreading experience. Reading focuses attention, eliminates distractions, and creates the conditions for tranquillity. Postreading experience is a moral testing-ground in which theory is applied to practice.

Augustine's approach to the comparable theme is presented in the *Confessions,* which was written between c.e. 397 and 401. As in Seneca and Quintilian, both of whom may have influenced his handling of the issues, reading plays an important role in the formation of character. Precepts from philosophy and philosophical maxims from the Bible are collected, memorized, and repeated. Augustine describes a type of internal meditation that employs personal memories rather than remembered maxims for the purpose of self-examination. The "text" in this case consists in the earlier life of the bishop himself, which is critically reviewed as if it were a narrative undergoing moral commentary. This was a bold step, which amounted to a positive reevaluation of stories as aids to moral philosophy—not a move sanctioned by the Platonism or Neoplatonism that he so much admired. Moreover, Augustine replaced mythical tales, as found for example in Homer, with the notion of a local, personal narrative as the privileged form of instruction. He invented the modern notion of autobiography as *Bildungsroman*, which was to have a long life in Western literature.

Augustine's *confessio* is both *vita* and spiritual exercise: it was conceived as a successor to the story of Aeneas's wanderings in the *Aeneid* and may even have been read aloud before an audience of potential converts, just as Roman schoolboys listened to recitation of Vergil's epic for entertainment and moral instruction. Within the *Confessions*, reading is looked upon in two distinctly Augustinian perspectives: it is a positive force, which can lead the individual to God by means of scripture, and a potentially negative force, since in his view readers, like speakers, can never be sure that the words they use accurately represent the realities they have in mind. Augustine is skeptical about his personal ability to hold to a course of action based on precepts that he has merely read about. He is not at all sure that abstractions can overcome the demands of the flesh: some of the most vivid episodes in the *Confession* document their failure to do so. In adopting reading as his major spiritual discipline, therefore, he does not abandon a regimen for controlling the body: he intends to reinforce it.

3

By 525, when St. Benedict founded a small monastery at Monte Cassino and wrote his *Rule*, ascetic reading was regularly practiced by religious communities in both the Greek and Latin branches of the church. The principal formula by which this technique of reading was known in the West in the following centuries is *lectio divina*.[29]

This term, which designates a combination of audible reading and silent meditation, is widely utilized during the centuries in which there are large pockets of Latin nonliteracy and numerous oral traditions flourishing in the western empire. As a consequence, references to *lectio divina* are normally situated in an oral context, whether the reading in question consists in the vocal and visual perusal of an unread written text or the readerly recitation of a known and remembered text.

The primary purpose of reading in this context is to promote virtuous thought and action, as does the cultivated reflection of pagan authors such as Cicero, Seneca, and Epictetus. Isidore of Seville (d. 636), who synthesizes patristic thinking on many subjects in his encyclopedic writings, speaks of the spiritual perfection that arises equally from *lectio* and *meditatio*. He advises the energetic reader (*lector strenuus*) that what is read is to be implemented (*ad implendum quae legit*) rather than to become an object of knowledge alone (*ad sciendum*).[30] In his opinion, reading is the successor to ancient *otium* as the culturally acceptable form of "spiritual leisure."[31] Another term for describing this type of reading is *sacra pagina*, which differs from *lectio divina* in being directed toward the meaning of the text.[32] A third expression that is employed from time to time in theological contexts is *sola scriptura*, which is utilized by Hugh of St. Victor (d. 1141)[33] and later reinterpreted by Luther as designating the reader's individual understanding of scripture in the absence of sanctioned interpretive guidelines.

Lectio divina and its cognates do not describe a method

of interpretation or hermeneutics but a slow, tranquil, and deliberative type of reading that is chiefly grounded in the voice of the reading subject. A much-quoted aphorism from a pseudo-Augustinian sermon sums it up this way:

> Deus nobis loquatur in lectionibus suis;
> Deo loquamur in precibus nostris.[34]
>
> [Let God speak to us in his readings;
> Let us speak to God in our prayers.]

In the ninth century, Smaragdus of St. Mihiel commented on this statement, stating:

> Orationibus mundamur, lectionibus instruimur. . . .
> Qui vult cum Deo semper esse, frequenter debet orare,
> frequenter et legere.[35]
>
> [By prayers we are cleansed, by readings we are instructed. . . . He who wishes to remain always with God should pray frequently as well as read frequently].

There are three principles involved in *lectio divina* that figure regularly in the sources by the early sixth century and continue to play a role in shaping the outlook of the ascetic reader for some time afterward: these are concerned with withdrawal, attention, and silence.

Throughout the late ancient and medieval periods, reading is viewed as a way of achieving a high degree of mental concentration, which requires withdrawal from potential distractions. In addition to aiding in the transmission of information recorded in the text, the focusing of attention brings about a desirable psychological transformation in the reader, opening a pathway to mental elevation and mystical enlightenment.

Although such reading does not normally take place silently, it is universally viewed as a preparation for meditative silence: not only for the environmental silence expressed by the transitive verb *tacere*, but for the experiential silence suggested by the intransitive verb *silere*. This is the absence of sound and movement that accompanies perfect inner tranquillity. One has to listen for silence, just as one learns to pay attention. Ambrose of Milan said that it was more difficult to learn how to be silent than to learn to speak. Augustine beautifully summed up the ancient lessons on attention and silence in the "vision at Ostia" in *Confessions* 9.10.25. Shortly before Monica's death, he and his mother withdrew into themselves and experienced a momentary vision of life after death. Their attention was awakened and deepened as words faded and silence prevailed: in the end it was the figure of Silence who addressed their metaphysical concerns.

The most important statements on silence among the Latin fathers were made by Gregory the Great, for whom wordlessness was given an expanded role in relating inner and outer religious experience.[36] Later, Hugh of St. Victor referred to three types of silence, corresponding to the historical development of humanity through periods dominated by natural law, written law, and the blessed life.[37] Eastern monasticism approached the subject from another angle. According to the doctrines of hesychasm, Symenon of Studion (d. 1022) proposed that a vision of God's uncreated light could be attained by means of ascetic practices in which silence played the major role. Proponents of this view at Mt. Athos included among the practices of hesychasm regular breathing (comparable to Buddhist mindfulness meditation) and the ritual repetition, followed by silence, of the prayer "Lord Jesus Christ, son of God, have mercy on me."[38] By the turn of the fourteenth century in the West, new dimensions were brought to the notion of silence and *lectio divina* by Eckhart (d. 1327), whose attempts to express the inexpressible were later redeployed by Romantic poets and philosophers influenced by the pantheistic implications of his mysticism.

The application of these principles gave rise to a large literary tradition of ascetic writings in the Latin West. By this is meant a set of recognizable genres such as prayers, confessions, saints' lives, dialogues, and religious poems, which gradually formed an autonomous, self-sustaining body of texts to which later authors looked for historical models.[39]

These writings provided the literary foundation for medieval as well as early modern experiments with meditation, including secular varieties, and lay the groundwork for the Western conception of the ascetic/aesthetic reader, which emerged in the late Middle Ages and the Renaissance.[40] Among the important examples of this union after 1100 are the *Sermons on the Song of Songs* of Bernard of Clairvaux (d. 1153), which utilize the sensual imagery of biblical originals to promote the puritan asceticism of Cistercian communities. A thirteenth-century variant is represented by the life and thought of Francis of Assisi (d. 1226): here the ascetic dimension is located in the *imitatio Christi*, while the aesthetic is re-created sensually and emotionally by the reading, listening, or visual audience. Francis wrote nothing beyond his admonitions, letters, *Rule*, and prayers (among them the lovely *Canticle to the Sun*, the first poem in Italian). But a vast corpus of tales, legends, miracles, prophecies, and paintings arose from the story of his life, which was passed on orally by the "three friends" and formally transcribed by Thomas of Celano. The relationship between a saint and his or her public was particularly important in conveying the message of sainthood,[41] and in distinguishing the ascetic sufferings of the holy figure from their aesthetic re-creation by his or her admirers.

The links between reading and asceticism during these centuries were influenced in many ways by changes in book production. Bibles copied after 1100 differ from those in earlier periods in format, page layout, word separation, punctuation, chapter divisions, methods for indexing, the use of diagrams, and in the occasional imitation of Psalter organization in Hebrew manuscripts.[42] While remaining medieval in their extensive use of abbreviation and localized scripts, these codices nonetheless begin to look superficially like the early printed Bibles of the fifteenth century. Parallel developments take place in aspects of the ascetic life that depend on the use of written materials, especially in prayers, meditations, and liturgy. For erudite readers, the format of sacred books permits the creation of longer, more complicated, analytically organized glosses, which give rise in their turn to the first medieval statements of systematic theology. For the masses, communication is facilitated by preaching, church wall paintings, and vernacular translations of the Bible. Even mysticism becomes more literary in expression, and mystical expressions spill over from religious to secular writings, reappearing in the love lyrics of Provençal and Italian poets.[43]

Authors incorporate into their writings a combination of the ascetic methods utilized in antiquity and late antiquity without necessarily distinguishing the historical periods in which they arise or the schools of thought to which they belong. An example of this adaptation takes place in the genre known familiarly as *"pensées,"* which is introduced into late ancient culture by Epictetus and Marcus Aurelius, Christianized by the desert fathers, and expressed in

different ways in Erasmus's *Adages* and Pascal's *Pensées*—
later completing its career in such works as the *Pensées* of
Joubert, the *Marginalia* of Coleridge, and Nietzsche's *Thus
Spake Zarathustra*. The major twelfth-century work of
this type is the *Meditations* of Guigo I of La Chartreuse
(d. 1136). "What strikes us first of all on reading [Guigo's
Meditations]," noted Etienne Gilson, "is their extraordi-
nary beauty."[44] In a pure, simple style, Guigo offers himself and his brethren a spiritual autobiography as a series of
sculpted *pensées*, which faithfully reflect the image of his
interior life. Here are a few quotations:

> [15] Longam tentationem petit, qui longam vitam petit.
> Tentatio enim est vita hominis super terram.
>
> [He who asks for a long life asks for a long trial. For the
> life of man on earth is a trial.]
>
> [17] Ideo tu tibi places, quia nihil te boni a te habere non
> intelligis.
>
> [You are satisfied with yourself because you do not un-
> derstand that you have nothing of good from yourself.]
>
> [19] Qui gaudet laudibus perdit laudes.
>
> [He who rejoices in praise loses praise.]

There are many echoes of the Stoic demand for control of
the emotions:

> [86] Nemo iratus beatus. Et e converso.
>
> [No angry man is happy: the converse too.]
>
> [91] Liberis liberatore opus non est.
>
> [The free man has no need of someone to free him.]

And the recommendation to free ourselves from illusions:

[105] [liberally paraphrased] We are always sure that we are doing well, whether we are or not; and, when things are not going smoothly, we frequently indulge in self-pity, which is not so bad either. In manufacturing these feelings for ourselves from the outside or the inside only one thing is certain: we all deceive ourselves.

Finally, on reading, one observation:

> [192] Quicquid legis in libris, potes videre oculis in hominibus, id est quid declines, et quid facias.
>
> [Everything that you read in books you can see in men's eyes, that is, what not to do and what to do.]

In addition to consolidating such traditions, the twelfth century was a time of transition, in which two types of reading were practiced, namely "monastic" and "scholastic." An example of these approaches is provided by Peter Abelard, who wrote ascetic treatises in which ancient meditative reading was recommended, among them the letter of direction addressed to Heloise at the Paraclete. As noted, the correspondence between the two lovers is modeled on an ancient spiritual exercise, the *Moral Epistles* of Seneca; and, in the *Ethica*, Abelard proposes a theory compatible with these writings in which emphasis is placed on the verbal assent of the individual in doing right or wrong. Yet it is not through this Augustinian conception of sin as a by-product of intentions that he deals with ethical issues in his mature theology: there he opts for the discursive, logico-deductive methodology of *Sic et Non*. The ascetic reading that is found in his spiritual letters places great weight on the subjective disposition of the reader, whereas the later method is concerned with accuracy in the reading and interpretation of a specific text and, subsequently, with the solution to the philosophical problems it raises. Hugh of St. Victor attempted to bridge these approaches in his *Didascalicon*, which is the first modern manual of reading and interpretation, as well as the earliest medieval book in which the term "reading" (*lectio*) is found in the title.

The twelfth century is likewise the point of departure for the consolidation of *lectio spiritualis* as a complement to *lectio divina*. The relationship between these types of monastic devotion and the difference between them can be illustrated by a pair of experiments. Suppose you are asked to repeat aloud a verse of a psalm with your eyes on the text and your mind fixed on the meaning of the words by means of verbal repetition. If you perform this task with attention, you will be close to the medieval discipline of *lectio divina*: you will be reading strenuously, as if performing a type of physical exercise, employing simultaneously the senses of sight and sound, feeling and hearing the words of the text as their meaning is understood, reminiscing and remembering the phrases as they are repeated aloud and mulled over in the mind.[45]

Then perform a second experiment. With the sound of the text still reverberating in your ears, close your eyes and concentrate on the inner development of your own reflections, following them as they proceed in an associative manner from the meaning of the text to other pious thoughts. In this case, your thinking may begin with the words of the psalm, as they are pronounced, but may find itself progressing through both words and images in other directions, by means of thematic associations. If you perform this task without permitting distractions, you will be close to *lectio spiritualis*. You will have proceeded from the monastic reading recommended by the Benedictine Rule to the spiritual reading practiced by Bonaventure in the *Itinerium Mentis in Deum* (1259) or by Julian of Norwich in the *Revelations of Divine Love* (after 1373).[46]

In both *lectio divina* and *lectio spiritualis*, but especially in the latter, there is a change in the function of attention. In normal reading, attention is focused on following the text in a passive and discursive fashion: passive, because the source of attention is external to the subject rather than actively taking shape within; and discursive, because the reader's thoughts are led from one item of information to another by means of the text, thus constituting a discourse that may continue in the mind after the text is put aside. Attention is frequently defocalized and intermittent, inasmuch as, during the period of reading, the mind wanders from the text to other matters. Such errancy can be determined by the content of the text but can also arise from other sources, for instance the subject's emotional state.

This form of attention, which is centrifugal, can be contrasted with the centripetal, focused attention that is taught in manuals of meditation for contemplatives in both East and West. This type of attention is nondiscursive, inasmuch as it depends on the subject's will rather than the text being read, and nonintermittent, inasmuch as distractions are allowed to pass through the mind without deflecting the subject's concentration. In this respect, advanced Christian contemplation has much in common with the striving for *apatheia* in Stoicism and with the differing techniques for preventing mental dispersal in Buddhism and Neoplatonism. It is by means of such concentrated attention, meditators believe, that a false, phenomenal self, which is created by the fluctuating impressions of disorganized consciousness, can be replaced by a true, nonphenomenological self, which manifests itself in consciousness as a nontemporal state of being.

Lectio spiritualis thus completes the transition begun in *lectio divina*, in which the project envisaged in the reading process moves from outer text to inner person.

The progress of the individual in search of this type of self-knowledge was aided by the use of visual imagery in meditation. Disfavored by Jewish and Muslim theologians and disputed within Byzantine Christianity, images nonetheless played a major role in ascetic thinking after late antiquity, when John of Damascus and Gregory the Great independently referred to such representations as a substitute for writing intended for those who could not read.[47] The question was addressed differently by the twelfth century in the West, when imagery and reading had become allied forces in religious meditation, images often simplifying, interpreting, and vividly re-creating important narrative events in scripture. During the thirteenth and fourteenth centuries wealthy people could afford private devotional books, which permitted the solitary reader to engage in such spiritual exercises alone. Also, visual aids were increasingly employed in churches for didactic purposes.[48] Images were easier to remember than texts (especially for nonliterates), and once recalled, the emotional associations of biblical writings could more easily fall into place, as in the stations of the cross (a series of fourteen pictures or carvings that depicted the last journey of Christ from Pilate's house to his entombment).[49] The tendency to think in images was given a philosophical foundation by the new account of vision that accompanied the study of Arabic and Aristotelian texts in the thirteenth century.[50] The ancient Greek intromissive theory was abandoned in the West, since lines of sight were no longer thought to pass from object to eye but from eye to object. Vision began to be studied scientifically as a dimension of human perception.

Still another change that had important consequences for asceticism was the rise of interest in writing as a complementary form of meditative activity, as noted in the case of Petrarch. This was not an entirely new development, since in earlier monastic culture the copying of manuscripts had been considered a valid form of manual labor and spiritual engagement. Also, the written word had long been a potent "school of silence," which was contrasted with the oral dialogue or disputation in monastic schools.[51] It was a short step to viewing composition as a type of contemplative practice in itself, even as an autonomous creative activity. The connection between writing, meditation, and literary composition was strengthened in the Devotio Moderna, which spread from Holland to parts of Germany, France, and Italy from the late fourteenth century. The movement's best-known contributions to ascetic and spiritual literature were the *Imitation of Christ* by Thomas à Kempis and the writings of Erasmus, who was educated by the lay Brethren of the Common Life in the decade after 1450.[52]

Other changes during this period include the increased accessibility to translations of religious writings among the laity and a shift in reading practices toward individual silent reading.[53] From the fourteenth century the meditative techniques of earlier periods were codified as a set of guidelines for ascetic reading, writing, and devotional practice. The most celebrated of these manuals is the *Spiritual Exercises* of Ignatius of Loyola, the founder of the Jesuit order, which was written shortly after a series of mystical experiences in 1522 and 1523. The purpose of this influential treatise was a series of rules for controlling the passions and surrendering oneself to God. Employing sense impressions, imagination, and understanding, Ignatius effectively synthesized some ten centuries of evolution in Christian spiritual thinking and introduced methods that were subsequently employed by authors of prose and poetry.

As a result of these changes, the period after the eleventh century experienced a rethinking of communicative strategies for relations between "texts" and "selves."[54] Differing in orientation from *lectio divina* or *lectio spiritualis*, but arising from a similar source, this type of reflection was more overtly literary in expression and, building on the Augustinian heritage, utilized reading in particular to explore subjectivity and intentionality. Reading generated a heightened awareness of the purposeful nature of all thinking, and as a consequence an interest in intentions became a major theme of philosophy between Anselm and Aquinas. At the same time, the reader's field of intentionality was restricted, owing to the necessity of concentrated attention, and readers began to employ flexible interpretive strategies for approaching questions related to the future rather than relying on external schemes for envisaging things to come such as divination, prophecy, or astrological prediction. In other words, the new awareness of textual culture and the reader's attention to text subjectively oriented thinking about the self, while the broadening of the range of intentionality through reading provided a theoretical justification for this orientation.

Typical of such reflections is the preface to the *Liber de Modo Bene Vivendi*, a twelfth-century Cistercian treatise indebted but not attributed to Bernard of Clairvaux, in which a monastic brother gives the following advice to a sister:

Receive this book, put it before your eyes like a mirror (*quasi speculum*), and think about it at all times like a source of reflection (*velut speculum*). For the precepts of God are mirrors, in which souls look into themselves and become acquainted with their faults . . . , since no one is free from failings; [a mirror] in which they correct the defects of their thoughts (*vitia cogitationum*); and in which, now ablaze with light, their countenances are united through the image that is reflected back. . . . Therefore, read this book, venerable sister, read it thoroughly, read it again and again. . . .[55]

Philip of Harvengt (d. 1183), a Premonstratensian canon, spoke of the intimacy acquired through reading, in his devotional work *De Silentio Clericorum*. He proposed that in meditative reading vocal conversation is restricted so that one can converse more familiarly with God in the secret of the heart (*in secreto cordis sui Deo familiarius colloquatur*), since the tongue is as silent as the inner mind is at peace (*nec quoties tacet lingua, totiesque interior animus conquiescit . . .*). This is not "the silence of the lips" or "the page" but a tranquillity that the reader "experiences . . . within."[56] In harmony with such views, Adam of Dryburgh (d. c. 1212) saw the spoken and literary discourse associated with the reading of sacred texts as the source of the soul's restoring, repairing, or re-creation (*Sermo quippe sacrae lectionis, animae refectio est*).[57] It is by means of reflective reading that the erudite and instructed individual can judge himself in the present (*homo . . . de deipso in praesenti possit judicare*),[58] and through conversation on the text's meaning that the hidden springs of his conscience can be revealed to others and to God.[59] We are enlightened by reading, expanded by action, inflamed by prayer (*Et lectio quidem illuminat; actio vero impinguat; oratio quoque inflammat*).[60] Garnier of Rochefort (d. c. 1225), another writer in this tradition, compared *cogitatio*, *meditatio*, and *contemplatio* in the following way:

Cogitatio is like a wanderer or voyager (*viator*), who goes from place to place looking for the right way but never sure what it is. *Meditatio* is the office of showing the way, after many deviations, to the right destination. *Contemplatio* is what takes place when one has come near the place one seeks; then, with the mind affected, one is dumfounded and wholly outside oneself.[61]

Garnier adds that "there are four motivations in the mind (*in animo . . . motus*). These are *ratio, sensualitas, aviditas,* and *devotio,*" which, acting in concert, determine styles of mental elevation and stabilize our thinking.[62]

Among these figures it was an earlier proponent of meditation, namely Odo of Cambrai (d. 1113), who prepared the ground for such reflections by taking a philosophical approach to the topic of the meditating self. Odo argued that we envisage many things in thought, and some of these take the form of figures in the mind.[63] In his view, a *persona* is an *individuum* possessing a rational nature: among the many things we call "individuals," however, only those enjoying reason are truly *personae*. In order to clarify this distinction, Odo proposes that a grammarian can speak of a *persona* in three ways: by what is said (*quae loquitur*), by what is communicated to someone else (*cui fit sermo*), and by the matter or message in the speech (*de quae fit sermo*). To the trio of speaker, listener, and independent meaning he then adds a fourth element, namely the discourse of reason itself (*locutionis ratio*), which differs from spoken speech just as a person's representation is distinguishable from reality. Odo suggests that an actor cannot imitate a living person unless he possesses this reason of speech to guide his movements. By implication all of us, going about our daily activities, are *personae* acting out roles, as we attempt to relate inner and outer discourses concerning the self. In Odo's rethinking of the Augustinian "inner word," there is more than a hint of a contemporary notion—the literary construction of consciousness.

One of the discoveries of twelfth-century writers on such themes is that the reader/thinker who is configured in their texts is never really alone. This period's statements on the topic of solitude reorient ancient reflection on the subject and prepare the way for the subtleties accompanying literary discourses on solitude in the following three centuries.[64] Religious authors are aware that the written text confers the illusion of solitude by forcing the reader to concentrate on his own thoughts; however, a distinction has to be made between this type of isolation, which is largely subjective in origin, and objective solitude, which in their view is the result of man's disobedience in Eden and his subsequent alienation from God. There is also a recognition in both lay and religious branches of society that some of the so-called objective sources of solitude are man-made. These consist in roles, norms, and relations of status that define the boundaries of legitimate participation in communities and effectively establish rules of inclusion or exclusion for individuals. The reading culture helps to set up these boundaries, which are as much about what medieval society intends to be as they are about what it is. It is this sensibility toward new sources of solitude that separates the meditations on the self in Augustine, who finds causality only in God, from those of his twelfth-century admirer Guibert of Nogent, who considers many types of causality—natural, supernatural, and human—but is convinced that he understands none of them.

4

In the final two sections of this lecture I would like to return to my point of departure and discuss schemes for ascetic reading that can be traced back to what I have said in

lecture one about Plato and Augustine. My example of the
Platonic approach is the description of the social function
of reading in Thomas More's *Utopia*, which is modeled on
the *Republic*. I offer two examples of Augustinian developments, since these are worked out differently in literature
and philosophy. The one is illustrated by selections from
English "metaphysical" poetry in the early seventeenth
century, the other by Descartes' *Meditationes*.

Plato is the earliest thinker who is concerned with the social consequences of ascetic readership. This theme is taken
up by More, whose desire to find an equilibrium between
ascetic and aesthetic designs is suggested in the title of the
1517 edition of *Utopia*, which characterizes his *libellus* as
a Horatian combination of entertainment and moral benefit.[65] The ascetic side is represented by a variant of Platonic
and monastic renunciation, namely freedom from possessions, which More's first reader, Guillaume Budé, traced to
Pythagorean origins,[66] but which More could have derived
from St. Ambrose.[67] In this light Budé contrasts the limitations of contract law, implicitly criticized in book 1 of
Utopia, with "the standard of truth and . . . the command
of the Gospel,"[68] which is charitable in purpose. This is a
thinly disguised echo of the contrast between law and spirit
in St. Paul.

Budé's letter also draws attention to a central feature of
More's utopian conception, which, like the book of Genesis,
frames its story of the discovery of morality within a highly
aesthetic landscape, namely the earthly paradise:

Utopia lies outside the limits of the known world. Undoubtedly it
is one of the Fortunate Isles, perhaps close to the Elysian Fields. . . .
It is . . . divided into many cities, but they all unite and harmonize
in one state, named Hagnopolis [a holy community]. The latter is
content with its own institutions and possessions, blessed in its

innocence, and leading a kind of heavenly life which is below the level of heaven but above the rabble of this known world.[69]

The role that reading will play in creating what Budé calls the "pattern of good life" on the island is hinted at by More, who prefaces book 1 with lines written in the Utopian alphabet in which it is claimed that a philosophical commonwealth (*civitas philosophica*) has been established without the need for philosophy (*philosophia*). More's epigraph, too, states that Utopia or Nowhere is a rival, even a victor, over Plato's design for the republic (*Nunc ciuitatis aemula Platonicae, / Fortasse uictrix*), the major reason being the superiority of the practical over the theoretical, as described by "men, works, and the finest laws."

Utopia's victory over its Platonic ancestor is reaffirmed by Peter Giles in his letter of 1516 to Jerome Busleyden, who compares More's fictional traveler, Hythlodaeus, to Ulysses in the extent of "his knowledge of countries, men, and affairs." Similar thinking is found in the response of John Desmarais of Cassel to Peter Giles, who notes, after reading More's text, that "whatever pertains to the good constitution of a commonwealth may be seen in it as in a mirror," as does Jerome Busleyden in his letter of 1516. The contrast between worldly affairs (*negotia*) and studious leisure (*literis*) is made in a different way by More himself, in his reply to Peter Giles, when he complains that his busy life leaves him little time for writing. The purpose of composing *Utopia* is to have it read and studied, first of all by his humanist friends, such as Peter, to correct errors, subsequently by the public, whom More later in the preface accuses of being victimized by poor education. It is the audience, then, that progresses along with More as he listens to Raphael's account of Utopian institutions.

The Platonic preference for philosophy over poetry is maintained in the description of this fictive personage, whose voyages are said to resemble the intellectual trajectories of Plato rather than those of Palinurus or Ulysses. A reasonable Latinist and advanced Hellenist, Raphael disdains Latin philosophy, "except certain treatises of Seneca and Cicero," a negative opinion echoed by the Utopians after their introduction to classical languages.[70] The conversation between More and Raphael takes place appropriately in a garden—the quintessential symbol of the lost Eden. Raphael recounts how, after the departure of Amerigo Vespucci, he and his companions traveled over a kind of desert, "a gloomy and dismal region . . . without cultivation or attractiveness." The voyagers then entered a countryside with a milder, more temperate climate, where they found a variety of cities, races, laws, and ways of life. In this narrative there are echoes of three earlier descriptions of a similar type, namely the arrival of Moses in the promised land, the discovery of Carthage by Aeneas, and the emergence of order from chaos in the allegorical poetry of Bernard Silvestris and Alan of Lille.

Raphael gave away his possessions to his friends and relatives in youth, thus adopting a life of voluntary poverty. Despite Peter Giles's arguments for entering public service, Raphael assures Giles and More that he is unwilling to surrender *otium* for *negotium*—study for affairs.[71] Nor does he believe that counseling rulers (*consilium*) serves any great purpose, since much of the political chatter that takes place at meetings between rulers and counselors has as its rationale the advancement of the adviser's material situation; even when it does not, there is no guarantee that the despot in question will pay attention to what is said. After a lengthy discussion of the problems of managing a state, Raphael concludes that Plato was right "in abstaining from administration of the commonwealth." Better for philosophers to remain detached from government, "since they cannot remedy the folly of others."[72]

There is some evidence, dating from his period in the Charterhouse, that More believed ascetic reading could contribute to overcoming the tension between material advancement and philosophical well-being that characterized his early career as a lawyer and counselor. The Utopians are presented as an alternative, since, in their "wise and holy institutions," there are no lawyers, "very few laws," and as a result "affairs are ordered so aptly that virtue has its reward."[73] At the root of their success lies a combination of political egalitarianism, shared obligations, and absence of ownership of property and means of production:[74]

This wise sage [i.e., Plato], to be sure, easily foresaw that the one and only road to the general welfare lies in the maintenance of equality in all respects. I have my doubts that the latter could ever be preserved where the individual's possessions are his private property. . . . I am fully persuaded that no just and even distribution of goods can be made and that no happiness can be found in human affairs unless private property is utterly abolished. While it lasts, there will always remain a heavy and inescapable burden of poverty and misfortunes for by far the greatest and by the best part of mankind.

With contemporary England's deplorable social conditions in the background of such a statement (rather than Plato's views in the *Republic*, where equality of possessions is granted only to the military elite),[75] ascetic reading enters the picture within Raphael's enthusiastic account of the Utopians' work ethic. The syphrogrants (two hundred officials, chosen from groups of thirty families, among whose functions are the election of regional governors) have as their chief responsibility to see that no one is idle (*ne quisquam desideat ocius*).[76] Each person practices his trade for six hours a day, three before and three after the noon meal. When they are not working, eating, or sleeping, the Utopians are at leisure: these periods cannot be spent in excess (*luxus*) or dilatoriness (*segnities*), but the citizens of the commonwealth are free to choose between their professional activities and intellectual pursuits, depending on their tastes and levels of education. Public readings (*publicae . . . lectiones*) normally take place before daybreak; however, they are required only for those who have chosen to specialize in the study of letters (*ad literas . . . selecti sunt*). Lectures are attended by many men and women who have an interest in learning, while others devote their leisure hours to the perfection of the arts they have mastered, since, More observes, they possess the type of mind that does not ascend easily to contemplative reflection within a given discipline (*quorum animus in nullius contemplatione disciplinae consurgit*).[77] But, in keeping with More's egalitarian views, they are no less valued in the commonwealth.

There are other forms of recreation, including music and conversation, and two demanding games, one based on competition by means of numbers, the other structured around a battle between virtues and vices.[78] But notably lacking in the Utopians' education is the literary, rhetorical, and historical reading of texts favored by Erasmus and his humanist friends, a type of reading that More defends against the alleged weaknesses of scholastic logic in his response to Martin Dorp. If Erasmus asks what it means to be a Christian, as a relationship between thought and action, the reading program of the Utopians outlines a methodology for making religion a way of life within a world that has distorted its original aims—a pertinent strategy, "if Christ's mission was, as Erasmus and perhaps More believed, the renewal of a nature once wholly good but corrupted by evil custom beyond the power of mere men to restore it."[79]

Here, then, as Budé suggested, is a people who seem to implement Christian charity without any formal knowledge of Christianity, as did some ancient philosophical sages. Where Erasmus and More differ is in the latter's unshakable belief in the value of asceticism as a component of this outlook, which deepens as his political position deteriorates and has its final expression in the spirituality of the Tower Works. As J. H. Hexter observes:

Utopia . . . is a society at once religious and austere. Its austerities, however, are not those of a withdrawn community of spiritual athletes performing special feats of self-mortification. . . . The austerities of Utopia are imposed on all Utopians, the laws of a commonwealth, not the rules of a cloister. . . . The laws for a holy commonwealth, of course; their vigor is the indispensable prop of social righteousness; the asceticism of Utopia is an asceticism of this world, an *innerweltliche Askese*. . . .[80]

More returns to the theme of education when speaking of the source of Utopians' moral virtue. This arises from their being raised (*educti*) in a society in which there is no need for material possessions and from their having early received training in the relevant doctrines and literate disciplines (*doctrina & literis*).[81] All men and women are given a certain level of education (*literis imbuuntur*), while a small number of people, who are singled out as children because of their personality, intelligence, and propensity for learning, are relieved of manual labor in order to devote themselves full-time to the acquisition of knowledge. The island's educational system is a mixture of classical elitism and humanist prejudice: the goal is mastery of inherited learning in Greek, Latin, and Hebrew, for which the Utopian language seems particularly well endowed. Medieval logic and scientific achievement are devalued in favor of amateur astrological prognostication. Yet a special place is reserved for philosophy, which is viewed in medieval fashion as a comprehensive discipline including ethics, music, dialectic, and arithmetic. More emphasizes that the Utopians are unacquainted with ancient thinking on these subjects before Raphael's arrival; yet all the classical questions are debated—good and evil, body and soul, virtue and vice, and the meaning of happiness.

Raphael marvels at the close connection between philosophy and religion, noting that the latter, like More's piety, is grave and severe, even sad and inflexible (*grauis & seuera . . . fereque tristis & rigida*).[82] Like the Christian Neoplatonist Augustine, on whom More lectured eruditely at St. Lawrence's Church, London, in 1501, the Utopians never discuss religion without drawing on rational arguments derived from philosophy. But their chosen pathway to the afterlife differs from what is outlined in *The City of God*, where the arbitrariness of grace is invoked, and resembles instead a combination of moderate Pelagianism and Thomistic influences, inasmuch as salvation is earned rather than bestowed and punishments are made appropriate to misdeeds. Also, unlike patristic and medieval thinkers, the Utopians have an uncomplicated theology, which requires a combination of rationality and metaphysics:

The principles are as follows: the soul is immortal (*immortalem*), and, owing to God's benefaction (*dei beneficentia*), born for happiness (*ad felicitatem*). After this life, rewards are determined for our virtues and good deeds and torments for our disgraceful actions. Although these principles are part of religion, [the Utopians] nonetheless reckon that it is by means of reason (*ratione*) that they are to be believed and adopted (*credenda & concedenda*).[83]

The narrator is critical of the Utopians' view that happiness (*felicitas*) is largely a question of pleasure (*voluptas*); this is defined as the motion or locus of the body and mind, which, when guided by nature, produces delight.[84] In describing the nature of pleasure More reveals a debt to ascetic notions found in writings on Epicureanism and Stoicism, for example in the *Moral Epistles* of Seneca. However, in the end he dissociates himself from central tenets of both systems. Unlike Epicureans, whose philosophy was rehabilitated during the early Renaissance,[85] the Utopians do not believe in the indifference of the deity; on the contrary, they are engaged monotheists, worshipping Mithras. The phrase *ad felicitatem*, with which Epicurean sentiments might be associated, does not only recall the source of such views in More, Cicero's *De Finibus*, but hints at Augustine's combination of Neoplatonic ascent and Christian intentionality, since the definition includes longing or striving for pleasure (*appetitio*). As in ancient Judaism and Christianity, there are pure ascetics among the Utopians, both celibate and married, who reject worldly pleasures, as well as priests of outstanding holiness (*eximia sanctitate*); these are men and women to whom young people are entrusted for their primary education in ethical matters.[86]

It is the Utopians' desire for "good and decent" rather than "false" pleasures[87] that prevents the soul from seeking enjoyment and avoiding discomfort without due consideration for consequences.[88] Unlike Stoics, Utopians do not subscribe to the view that virtue consists in living according to nature (*secundum naturam uiuere*).[89] True, they agree that the local function of reason is to guide our decisions, desiring or avoiding a course of action, but they also believe in a higher global purpose for reason, which "incites mortals in love and veneration for the Divine Majesty."[90] In this context the search for pleasure is influenced chiefly by altruism: "[Reason] reminds them and strongly encourages them to lead a life as free of anxiety and as full of joy as possible; and, because of the nature of fellowship (*pro naturae societate*), to help others to attain that end."[91] In the Utopians' religion, therefore, an ascetic design is framed within a doctrine of charity. While practicing austerities, individuals take account of the poverty and suffering of others; and they look beyond these actions to their potential moral consequences as helping or hindering their pursuit of happiness.[92]

Raphael notes their preference for pleasures of the mind (*uoluptates animi*), while admitting the value of pleasures arising from the senses, the body, and good health. The chief mental enjoyments consist in the exercise of virtue and the conscious awareness of the good life (*ab exercitio uirtutum bonaeque uitae conscientia*). The Utopians are convinced that this is the highest goal sanctified by religion.[93] Moreover, in spite of their commitment to manual labor, they remain indefatigable in their devotion to studies (*animi studijs infatigata*). Accordingly, when they hear from their visitors about the literature and learning of the Greeks (*de literis & disciplina Graecorum*), they turn up eagerly for public classes. Raphael recalls:

We started, therefore, to read with them (*coepimus ergo legere*). . . . They began so easily to imitate the shapes of the letters, so readily to pronounce the words, so quickly to learn by heart, and so faithfully to reproduce what they had learned that it seemed miraculous to us. The explanation is that most of them were already scholars. . . . In less than three years they were perfect in the language and able to peruse good authors without any difficulty unless the text had faulty readings.[94]

On a return voyage Raphael brings with him works of numerous classical authors, chiefly in the disciplines of philosophy, literature, history, and medicine: Plato and Aristotle; Homer, Aristophanes, Euripides, and Sophocles; Thucydides and Herodotus; and Hippocrates and Galen. The Europeans subsequently teach the Utopians the arts of papermaking and printing. More becomes the first author to connect the pursuit of happiness with the progress of a reading culture, indeed, with the mechanization of that culture. In this respect he differs from his chief mentor on the theme of virtue, happiness, and literary studies: *Utopia* does not reiterate Plato's plan for the education of the guardians in the *Republic* by means of moral narratives. Although *Utopia* book 2 is a story, the Utopians themselves are not taught by such tales but by "principles" in philosophy and religion, more closely resembling ancient Jews rather than Christians, for whom the narratives of the Gospels are paramount in importance. Moreover, when they finally learn about Christ, what they admire is "his disciples' common way of life," which, it is claimed, "is still in use among the truest societies of Christians."[95] There is a connection in Raphael's mind between monastic communism and the notion of communion.

Narrative nonetheless enters More's thinking from another direction. The story told by Raphael in book 2 of *Utopia* is a response to the formal dialogue in the *Republic*: as noted, it is also a commentary on the notion of lost but recoverable happiness in Christian tradition. In his thinking on this theme More is closer to Erasmus than to Augustine, since he genuinely believes that progress can be made toward salvation in this life, and, as humanist, that this progress can be brought about by a combination of classical and Christian education. Also, in his rescripting of the paradise myth, More changes Augustine's priorities as first outlined in the *Confessions* and later restated in *The City of God*. In Augustine's view, the discovery of truth is a consequence of learning Latin and Greek, the sacred languages in which the Old and New Testaments are transmitted to believers. By contrast, More poses the problem of other cultures, which have truths expressed in their own languages—languages that Europeans know nothing about. It is ironic, therefore, that the Utopians anticipate and in some cases improve upon the wisdom of the ancients, as transmitted in Western tradition. Their language appears to be no less capable than Greek or Latin for expressing eternal cultural values: in its flexibility and expressiveness, it can even be considered an alternative language of paradise.

5

I now turn to the Augustinian heritage, which differs in the manner in which it is worked out in literature and philosophy. This division is a consequence of different periods of consolidation in Augustinian methods employed by ascetic readers and writers. One of these is bounded by the late eleventh and twelfth centuries, while the other runs from the fourteenth to the early sixteenth.

Augustine's influence is intermingled, as noted, with that of the *Spiritual Exercises* of Ignatius, which bridges the medieval and Renaissance theory of meditation. This work had a powerful affect on religious writings in Spain, notably on Theresa of Ávila, whose *Life*, *Way of Perfection*, and *Interior Castle* were written between 1562 and 1577, and on the mystical poetry of her admirer, St. John of the Cross, who died in 1591. Another important literary inspiration was drawn from Francis of Sales (d. 1622), whose *Introduction to the Devout Life* and *Treatise on the Love of God* invited his readers to leave behind their transitory selves as a point of departure for a more complete abandonment of the self in God. Augustinian, Salesian, and Ignatian forces acting in concert deepened the spiritual dimension of the period's "metaphysical poetry" in authors such as John Donne (d. 1631) and George Herbert (d. 1633), as well as in Richard Crashaw, Andrew Marvell, Henry Vaughan, and Thomas Traherne.[96]

The English poetry of this period illustrates another aspect of the diversified development of ascetic reading after the twelfth century, namely the rise of national traditions. The origin of this phenomenon dates from the selective reception of Augustine's works in northern France and England after the eleventh century. In France, their effect was chiefly felt in spiritual writings and formal theology, whereas in England a century and a half later there was a comparable influence on secular literature. This took place following Chaucer's translations of the lyric poems of Petrarch, which were indebted to Augustinian techniques of meditation. In contrast to the French experience, in which the study of Augustine's writings played a role in the period's Latin "renaissance," in England the Augustinian tradition made its appearance in both Latin and vernacular writings; the latter included the spiritual works of Walter Hilton, Richard Rolle, Julian of Norwich, and Marjorie Kempe.

It was from these two streams, the one mediated by Petrarch, the other by the bishop of Hippo himself, that English literary Augustinianism gradually arose. When this insular tradition resurfaced in the seventeenth century and intermingled with spiritual works such as the *Spiritual Exercises* of Ignatius, it was already three centuries old. It is not surprising, therefore, that poets who engage in literary meditations in this period do so with a high degree of sophistication. What characterizes this poetry is a combination of Augustinian simplicity, informality, and directness, and a more rigorous visual and sensory experience, which can be associated with Ignatian methods. Both are found in George Herbert's "The Reprisall:"[97]

> I have consider'd it, and finde
> There is no dealing with thy mighty passion:
> For though I die for thee, I am behinde;
>   My sinnes deserve the condemnation.
>
> Oh make me innocent, that I
> May give a disentangled state and free:
> And yet thy wounds still my attempts defie,
>   For by thy death I die for thee.
>
> Ah! was it not enough that thou
> By thy eternall glorie didst outgo me?
> Couldst thou not griefs sad conquest me allow,
>   But in all vict'ries overthrow me?
>
> Yet by confession will I come
> Into thy conquest. Though I can do nought
> Against thee, in thee I will overcome
>   The man, who once against thee fought.

What the reader notes from the outset of this spiritual lyric is the simplicity and directness of the speaking "I," which, unlike Petrarch's "io," reflects clarity rather than complexity, and has a long rather than short perspective on the author's fluctuating emotions. For Petrarch, as noted, the chief theme of poetic engagement is the sentiment of exile, wandering, and circularity, in view of the impossibility of attaining both earthly and heavenly love, whence the opposites of emotion that are played out in his lyrics. In Herbert a different scenario is enacted: in contrast to Laura's emotions, which Petrarch cannot know, Herbert is sure of Christ's "mighty passion"; and it is this overwhelming sense of another's sacrifice on his behalf that tempers his expression of his own feelings in the poem's three last stanzas. Herbert seeks "abandonment," first for the self ("O make me innocent"), then for history ("I will come/Into thy conquest"). As in Augustine, this confession is not sacramental but autobiographical, and as in Petrarch, it is expressed through poetry rather than prose. Yet, whereas Augustine, through grace, submits completely, abandoning language with the world, and whereas Petrarch, through earthly love, cannot submit completely, as Francis/Petrarch tells Augustinus in the *Secretum*, Herbert invites the reader by means of poetry to use language to move toward the nonlanguage of spiritual truth.

My second brief illustration of seventeenth-century developments in ascetic reading is Descartes, who exemplifies an aspect of the French tradition of Augustinian influences, after Anselm of Canterbury, namely the philosophical.

Descartes called his major reflective work *Meditationes de prima philosophia*: the full title in translation is "Meditations on first philosophy in which the existence of God and the immortality of the soul are demonstrated." Recall that these are the problems taken up by Augustine in the *Soliloquies* as he debates with his faculty of Reason.[98] In reintroducing the concept of the soliloquy Descartes links two terms that had not occurred previously in Latin philosophy, namely "meditation" and "demonstration." By demonstration (*demonstrare*) he means "showing" by means of logical proof; by meditation (*meditatio*), he means a combination of two classical senses of the verb *meditor*, namely "to muse, consider, or meditate" and "to study, exercise, or practice,"[99] both of which were widely utilized in *lectio divina*.[100]

The exercises to which Descartes alludes were reasonably common in seventeenth-century thought. He acquired his knowledge of meditation at the Jesuit college of La Flèche, where the instruction manuals included both Augustine and Ignatius of Loyola. As envisaged by the Jesuits, *meditatio* was a discursive reflection involving logic and rhetoric by which the resources of reason and imagination were enlisted in applying the principles of the Christian life. This exercise required concentrated attention for about an hour a day, or alternately formal retreats in which there were longer periods of meditation. The reading was a fused tradition consisting of elements from *lectio divina* and *lectio spiritualis*: the slow, often interrupted perusal of a few texts, as well as the verbal and imaginative contemplation of their significance. Descartes refers to this training in his preface to the reader, where he advises no one to take up his text who is not prepared to meditate seriously along with the author: these are persons who can detach their minds from the incessant traffic of the senses and release their thinking from habitual prejudice. Such readers, he estimates, are few in number; yet only they will perceive the principles of order that guide his thinking (*rationes*) and their interconnection (*nexus*).[101] This is Augustine's Neoplatonic elitism reexpressed in seventeenth-century language.

The meditations of Descartes are the modern philosophical enactment of another ancient exercise, the retreat into solitude. Descartes' abandonment of the world is the philosophical equivalent of Weber's "world-renouncing" asceticism. As in the case of St. Antony's departure from Alexandria, Descartes' mental isolation permits him a new perspective on the world with which he is already familiar.

This is not a religious perspective, as in the case of Bernard, Francis, or Ignatius, but involves a comparable detachment from sense perceptions. It is by means of meditative withdrawal that Descartes fashions a new understanding of the natural world that he has left behind, just as religious thinkers reconfigured the fallen world of the senses after the departure of the first couple from the garden of Eden. Descartes describes this self-imposed isolation in terms that recall Augustine's description of his attempts to find time for leisured reflection in Milan and at the country retreat of Cassiciacum: "Fortunately, the day came when I was able to free my mind from cares and to manage to find some guaranteed leisure time. Alone, I withdrew: at last I felt free, and was able to devote my time seriously to the general demolition of my unproven views."[102]

In Descartes' transformation of this attitude, asceticism is retained, but on first view the reader appears to be absent. Descartes is aware that Augustine deliberately pictures himself as a reader/thinker in the narrative books of the *Confessions*, as he slowly acquires the knowledge and spiritual skills that permit him to transcend the world of reading and writing. But he seems to repudiate this method. His "meditations" do not progress through specific schools of thought, as do Augustine's; on the contrary, in order to prepare himself for his solitary reflections he has to clear his mind of the debris left behind by years of formal education. This is the book learning that he recalls Socratically in the *Discours de la méthode*, which was the source of "so many doubts and errors that the effort to instruct myself had no effect other than the increasing discovery of my own ignorance."[103]

But here, as in the works of figures like John Cassian and Guigo the Carthusian, the reader is not absent but has merely been disguised. Descartes makes use of a topos of early Christian education, which he could have learned from Antony, Augustine, or the life of St. Benedict by Gregory the Great, namely the refusal of worldly erudition in favor of teaching from within. Unlike Augustine, who uses this trope to prepare the way for inner instruction by Christ, he wants to find the answers to fundamental questions in both physics and theology by means of knowledge arising logically within himself. In both Augustine and Descartes, therefore, the audience is engaged in a process of education that leads from initial error, based on inherited teaching, to enlightenment: Augustine calls this *illuminatio* and Descartes *méthode*. The two are convinced that essential truths are self-evident: in Descartes, this is a single, irrefutable truth; in Augustine, numerous truths. Yet in each the "cogito" of the isolated thinker engaged with his thoughts is the model for philosophical investigation. Logical proof is a way of demonstrating to oneself what one already knows: in Augustine, this is knowledge imparted by God; in Descartes, knowledge derived from reasoned arguments that arise in the mind alone.

After the *Confessions*, Augustine rarely used the soliloquy for intellectual inquiries, preferring traditional Christian genres of sermon, commentary, and polemical treatise. He did not employ this method in his late masterpiece, *The City of God*; he abandoned it along with the tenets of ancient philosophy to which he adhered in his youth. By contrast, Descartes was convinced that the internal dialogue is the only way to establish true, irrefutable knowledge. The reader enters this universe of discovery through his invitation to participate in the thinking in which he is actively engaged. He does not ask the putative audience to summarize his arguments or to provide a systematic statement of his views, but to follow him as he leads the reader/thinker in a series of logico-meditative steps toward self-enlightenment and self-knowledge. Augustine, in exchanging the classical, exterior dialogue for the interior soliloquy, asks his readers to engage in rational dialogues with themselves in order to discover the movements of their souls and through these the reflection of God's image in themselves. By contrast, the *Meditationes*, which also consist of soliloquies, tackle these issues through philosophy alone.

Like Augustine, Descartes fashions a literary *persona* in order to do this: the fictive "I" (*je*) of the *Meditationes*, which is the equivalent of the first-person voice of Augustine in the *Confessions*. He sums up his technique at the beginning of meditation 3, where he relates how he prepares himself for his inner discourse:

I now close my eyes, I stop up my ears, I withdraw from my senses, I erase from my thinking all images of corporeal things, or, since this is difficult to do, at least I judge them of no worth, being useless and false. Conversing alone with myself and looking into myself more closely, I try to make myself a little better known and familiar to myself. For I am a thinking thing: that is, doubting, affirming, negating, understanding little, ignoring much, willing, denying, imagining, and even sensing.

If this statement reads like a combination of Plotinus and Augustine, it nonetheless highlights a central difference between the late ancient and Cartesian approaches to establishing truth. In Augustine, the exercise is a complement to the affirmation of existence, whereas in Descartes the logical proof for self-existence is argued independently of the meditative state in which it takes place. It is this, more than the proof itself, that marks Descartes as an early modern thinker.

3   The Aesthetic Reader

In my first lecture I described "the reader's dilemma," which arises from the difficulty of separating ascetic and aesthetic approaches to literary texts in the Western tradition. In the second lecture I presented a brief outline of the development of ascetic reading between the ancient and early modern periods. In my final lecture I discuss aesthetic reading and the creative imagination.

Let me begin by asking what is meant by aesthetic reading in an ethical context. The classic answer is given by Horace in a well-known statement at *Ars Poetica*, vv. 333–334:

> *Aut prodesse volunt aut delectare poetae*
> *aut simul et iucunda et idonea dicere vitae.*

> [Poets aim either to benefit, or to amuse,
> or to utter words at once both pleasing and helpful to
> life.][1]

Writing between 23 and 20 B.C.E., Horace is speaking about relations between the creative imagination, from which the pleasure of poetry is derived, and the benefits of literary experience, which include pleasure but also have something to do with the shaping of the reader's ethical outlook. He sums up his view of this connection a few lines earlier, when he proposes that

Scribendi recte sapere est et principium et fons. (v. 309)

[The origin and source of writing correctly is wisdom.][2]

The *Ars Poetica* is one of the rare works of classical Latin poetry that was studied continuously throughout the ancient, medieval, and Renaissance periods. Medieval authors frequently referred to Horace as *ethicus*, that is, "the moralist." The ninth-century Roman breviary included hymns in Horatian meters. In the twelfth century Metellus of Tegernsee, a Bavarian imitator of classical verse, composed seventy poems in honor of St. Quirinus, his monastery's patron, modeled on the four books of odes. Hugh of St. Victor quoted the *Ars Poetica* in his introduction to the study of scripture in order to remind his readers of the value of pre-Christian teachings on the virtues, which the Bible brings together under the rubric of charity.[3] Dante placed *Orazio satiro* among the seven great poets of antiquity,[4] while Petrarch created his sixty-seven *epistole* along the lines of the poet's verse epistles. In his *Defence of Poesy*, published in 1595, Sir Philip Sydney, recognizing that Plato is "the enemy of poets," proposed that "poesy . . . is an art of imitation, for so Aristotle termeth it in the word μίμησις, that is to say, a representing, counterfeiting, or figuring forth—to speak metaphorically, a speaking picture—with this end, to teach and to delight."[5]

In order to trace the evolution of the program that Horace had in mind, it is necessary to go beyond the statement on the pleasure and profit of poetry to which Sidney is referring and to say a few words about a development that was at work in Horace's time on which he himself was largely silent. This, as noted, was the emergence of a reading culture, which had been taking shape in Graeco-Roman civilization from the third century B.C.E. By the time Horace died, some eight years before the birth of Christ, this culture was already displaying the features by which it would be characterized in late antiquity and the Middle Ages.

The role played by reading in the final phase of Hellenistic education is not reflected in the language of the *Ars Poetica*. When Horace talks about poetry, he has oral performances in mind; and when he refers to ethical issues, as he does from time to time, he is thinking perhaps nostalgically of the manner in which they were openly debated in the ancient schools of philosophy, rather than as they appeared in the summaries, transcripts, and textbooks in the field that were routinely employed by instructors in his day. By the time he wrote, the venerable performances and interchanges that he had in mind were being generously complemented by public lectures and private reading. Older types of oral discourse were still very much alive, for example in legal oratory,[6] but it was the reader, teacher, and commentator who had become the common denominator of a trilingual culture (Greek, Latin, and Hebrew) in the Mediterranean world. The environment of reading expanded throughout late antiquity, culminating in the biblical translations and commentaries of Jerome, in which all three languages are drawn upon.

In the *Ars Poetica*, Horace suggests that poetry can help its readers to live a well-balanced, rewarding, and fulfilled life. He does not view literature as a rival for philosophy but as an introduction or a complement to philosophy—referring to philosophical doctrines as well as to the rhetorical and philological grounding of a civic layperson's way of life. On this view, reading and reflecting on literary texts can contribute to the ancient quest for happiness, *eudaimonia*. Horace agrees with Plato that poetry works by means of images, which in turn work on minds and emotions, although he nowhere states this view as a theory. But he does not believe that a poem is constructed of transitory impressions from which the permanence of ethical truths cannot be derived. On the contrary, he echoes the opinion of ancient educators, including Isocrates, Cicero, and his younger contemporary, Seneca, who propose that literature has the capacity to transcend these limitations and offer guidance on ethical matters. Implicit in the statements of such authors is the view that a good poem is a kind of truth unto itself, "goodness" in this context referring to literature that measures up to its announced and acknowledged aesthetic criteria.[7]

If such literature provides instruction about what constitutes aesthetically acceptable style, through meter, rhythm, and diction, there is a comparable harmoniousness in the constitution of other sorts of goodness, among them the pursuit of wisdom.

In Horace's opinion, Socrates' argument concerning the immorality of the gods is not an adequate response to the stylistic beauty with which their deeds are recorded by Homer or Vergil.[8] The aesthetic principles on which epic poetry is based are uninfluenced by the moral status of the characters who appear in them. It is possible to have a good epic written about the deeds of a bad person as takes place much later by means of Satan in Milton's *Paradise Lost*. Such a poem can teach something important about virtue by means of unvirtuous conduct. In contrast to Plato, who, if taken literally, wishes to substitute anodyne tales for gripping and instructive epic verse, Horace argues that we are best persuaded to adopt laudable courses of action by the literary and poetic power of what we see, hear, and feel. During the Renaissance a similar argument is brought against Augustine's criticism of Homer's immorality by humanists between Lorenzo Valla and Erasmus, who suggest that one cannot be a good Christian without an adequate understanding of the principles of style in classical Greek and Latin literature.

2

At the basis of Horace's statements is the assumption of a positive connection between ethics and the literary imagination. This thesis argues that poetic images may be false, inasmuch as they are merely representations of realities, but that such temporary mental creations can teach abiding truths. One can learn about ethics from literature, even while admitting, as Plato said, that literature consists mostly in imaginative concoctions. In this part of my lecture I explore what this paradoxical statement means to some thinkers before and after Horace.

The early history of the relationship between ethics and literary imagination can largely be told through the philological evolution of a single Greek term: φαντασία.[9] The noun, "making visible," is derived from φαίνειν, "to show." The word was transliterated into Latin and appears in English from the sixteenth century as the concept of "phantasy," which refers to "the mental apprehension of an object of perception," to "an illusory appearance," or more generally to "imagination," that is, "the process, faculty, or result of forming representations of things not present." The last definition is close to the view of Samuel Johnson, to which I refer later, as well as to the contemporary sense of "imagination," derived from Latin *imaginatio*, which makes its appearance in late authors such as Pliny and Tacitus. As it comes into English, imagination means "the action of forming a mental concept of what is not actually present to the senses," "the power which the mind has of forming concepts beyond those derived from external objects," or "the creative faculty" in poetry and other literary compositions.[10] By the eighteenth century the connotative fields of "phantasy" and "imagination" considerably overlap.

The ancient history of the word *phantasia* can be divided into successive phases.[11] There is a Greek segment, in which the pertinent questions are philosophical, even though rhetorical issues are not entirely neglected. This part of the story is represented principally by Plato, Aristotle, the Stoics, and some Neoplatonists. The second segment takes place in both Greek and Latin: here the main authors are Cicero, Plutarch, Seneca, Longinus, Quintilian, Philostratus, Boethius, and Augustine. In these writers philosophical matters are raised for discussion, but mostly as footnotes to what has come before; the major preoccupation is with the literary and visual arts and through them with what is nowadays called "the creative imagination."[12] These authors transcend the philological discussion of *phantasia* and begin to ask a modern question: What does an artist or writer do when he or she brings into being a work of art based on a preexisting mental image of what it should be like? And what are the ethical implications of that process for other types of "modeling" or "imitation" in life?

It was Plato who first raised the problem of *phantasia*, chiefly in the *Republic, Theaetetus,* and *Sophist.* His reflections arose from the ambiguity of *aisthesis,* which can refer to sensation or sense perception.[13] He concluded that a *phantasia,* when viewed as a "perception," operates at a higher level than when viewed as a "sensation," even though perceptions are derived from sensations. Whenever we ask ourselves what are the objects of our sense impressions, and how one object is similar to another or dissimilar from it, we employ our senses as well as our minds when we think about and attempt to judge what we perceive.[14] As argued in the *Theaetetus*, the ascertaining process takes place by means of an internal dialogue within the soul: questions and answers, affirmations or denials, resulting in an opinion, *doxa*.[15]

The terms that Plato uses to describe this process are *logos* and *legein*, the latter of which is the predecessor of the Latin *legere*, to read. Plato speaks of "dialogic" activity in the mind, which gives rise to an internal conversation, a process that is reinvented centuries later by Augustine, who is the first Latin to refer to these conversations as "soliloquies" (*soliloquia*).[16] In Plato's view, we cannot use the term "knowledge" to characterize our awareness of objects in which there is no discourse of this kind. But where there is discourse, there has to be a product. It follows that *phantasia*, although presented largely in negative terms in his dialogues, indicates the presence of a type of knowledge, and this knowledge, which is a combination of sense perception and judgment, is realized through inner speech.

In two places in his dialogues Plato talks about writing and painting as dimensions of imaginative activity. The best-known statement occurs near the end of the *Phaedrus*, where in a much-commented speech Socrates attacks writing's externality, claiming that

it will introduce forgetfulness into the soul of those who learn it: they will not practice using the memory because they will put their trust in writing, which is external and depends on signs that belong to others, instead of trying to remember from the inside, completely on their own. . . . They will imagine that they have come to know much while for the most part they will know nothing.

Painting is included in this condemnation, since "writing shares a strange feature with painting. The offsprings of painting stand there as if they were alive, but if anyone asks them anything they remain most solemnly silent. The same is true of written words. . . ."[17]

The less well-known contribution to the discussion is in the *Philebus*, where Socrates asks how things that we see and remember are judged true or false. His answer is that we can debate the matter with others or within ourselves, as suggested in the *Theaetetus*. If we adopt the second approach, the dialogue that takes place in the soul can be compared to the writing of a book: "If memory and perception concur with other impressions at a particular occasion, then they seem to me to inscribe words in our soul, as it were. If what is written is true, then we form a true judgement and a true account of the matter." Furthermore, two types of craftsmen are at work: one records what we think we see, while the other, like an artist, "follows the scribe and provides illustrations of his words in the soul."[18]

There is nothing in these assertions that contravenes what is said in the *Republic* about the falseness of poetic or artistic representations as imitations. Yet in two respects Plato lays the groundwork for more positive thinking on ethics and the literary imagination. First, imagination involves inner discourse, which is like writing or painting. By implication, writing and painting are types of inner discourse, as late ancient, medieval, and Renaissance thinkers sometimes suggest. Secondly, and more controversially, verbal understanding based on reasoning (*logos*) is judged to be prior to images, while at the same time images formed in the mind function as illustrations or complements of words. Finally, although Socrates formally repudiates writing because of its detrimental effect on memory, Plato subtly rehabilitates writing by configuring a hypothetical type of discourse that has features of both oral and written discourse.

There is still another element in Plato's thinking on the subject that should be mentioned in this context, although it does not arise in these writings: this is the notion put forward in the *Timaeus* that God is the supreme artist, who created the universe according to a prearranged plan. Using the *Timaeus* as their guide, Christian thinkers between late antiquity and the sixteenth century maintain that the most beautiful thing imaginable is God's Word; and the most perfect aesthetic object is the created world, ruled by humans. A secular version of this doctrine, to which reference is made later in this lecture, reappears during the Romantic period, when it is assumed by thinkers such as Herder, the Schlegels, and Coleridge that poetry and philosophy normally work together in artistic or literary creation. As one commentator notes: "The interdependence of . . . poet and philosopher was one of [Coleridge's] favorite tenets. Plato's philosophy was 'poetry of the highest kind.' 'Plato' . . . 'was a Poetic Philosopher, as Shakspeare was a Philosophic Poet;' and 'from Shakspeare to Plato, from the philosophic poet to the poetic philosopher, the transition is easy.'"[19]

I mention in passing two important criticisms of Plato's position that were influential on later ancient thinking about *phantasia*.[20] One arises from Aristotle's rejection of Plato's view of art as *mimesis* and his objections to the doctrine of forms, both of which have implications for the notion of *phantasia*.[21] For Aristotle, in *De Anima* and elsewhere, the main question does not concern the relationship between *phantasia* and reality, however that is defined, but between *phantasia* and its psychological stimulus.[22] Also, Aristotle severs Plato's connection between *phantasia* and *doxa*: the problem arises from the fact that an impression can be true as sensed but false as judged, for example, the visual appearance of the sun, which is perceived to be a tiny object in the sky but is in reality larger than the other planets. In general Aristotle has a more complex understanding than Plato of how, and in what conditions, *phantasiai* can be products of sense perceptions, even though he leaves many aspects of his account incomplete, for example, on the functions of time and memory. His discussion of *phantasiai* nonetheless includes the examination of waking states as well as sleep, visions, dreams, hallucinations, and madness. His view that insights into imagination can be gained from studying physiological states was subsequently taken up by Galen, Arab commentators, and, based on eighteenth-century experiments, by Coleridge.

By contrast, Stoic authors criticized Plato chiefly on epistemological grounds. They agreed that *phantasiai* are subjective states but were convinced that these states play an important role in the acquisition of knowledge. The relevant thinking developed out of the notion of *phantasia kataleptike*, that is, an impression literally stamped on the mind in accordance with an existing object of such a kind as cannot be derived from a nonexistent object.[23] This was contrasted with a noncataleptic fantasy, a mental impression that bears only an imprecise relation to an antecedent reality.[24] From this pair of concepts derived the distinction between "imaginative," as a creative component of thought, and "fantastic," as derivative and possibly misleading. Gerard Watson, who studied this theme down to the first century C.E., argued that the Stoics combined Plato's *phantasia*, as mixture of *aisthesis* and judgment, with Aristotle's statements on images, thus giving *phantasia* "a central place . . . in the process of human thought and language."[25]

After Stoicism, further changes in the meaning of *phantasia* take place toward the end of the Hellenistic period and in late antiquity. In both Greek and Latin the word evolves from a technical term in philosophy, as discussed by Sextus Empiricus and Epictetus, to the range of meanings of the English word "phantasy" or, as suggested later in this lecture, to something like Coleridge's term "fancy." The questions asked by philosophers give way to rhetorical, literary, and artistic concerns (with the exception of Johannes Scottus Eriugena in the ninth century, who revives ancient philosophical concerns surviving in Greek and Latin patristic thought).[26] The central conceptual issue is the same as in Plato, namely the nature of *mimesis*, but interest shifts from realities, as the source of impressions, to representations themselves, their nature, classification, and aesthetic qualities, which are explored by such authors as Quintilian and Plutarch. It is this development that gives rise to the much-discussed problem of "representing reality" through literature.[27]

As a consequence of this eclectic tradition of thinking on the topic of *phantasia*, works on imitation are no longer principally concerned with questions of truth and falsehood but with the creative imagination and its literary or artistic expression. Among commentators in late antiquity two figures stand out in the range of their interests and grasp of classical principles. One is Longinus, a hellenized Jew living in the first century C.E., whose short seminal book, *On the Sublime*, distinguishes between rhetorical and poetic fantasies and offers new directions for the understanding of emotion and imagination in Greek literature. The other major figure is Augustine, who is the most influential thinker on the creative imagination between the late fourth century and the thirteenth, when Aristotle's *Rhetoric* and *Poetics* become available in Latin through Greek and Arabic channels, the latter augmented by the contributions of Arab thinkers.[28]

Augustine was convinced that the human mind is capable of forming three types of images. These are images of things experienced through the senses, called *phantasiae*; images in the mind formed on the basis of report, called *phantasmata*; and images concerned with numbers, dimensions, or concepts such as wisdom, beauty, or justice, for which he had no technical term.[29] There is nothing new in this characterization of images from an ancient standpoint, except in Augustine's insistence that these are all memory images. Unlike Plato, who ascribed many types of memories to the doctrine of reminiscence, Augustine argued that all memories, including those for disciplines like geometry (Socrates' example in the *Meno*) are particular and individual. The central problem in the study of memory images does not concern the faculty of memory, which is unknowable, but the nature of remembering, which Augustine believed can be studied by means of introspection.[30]

Augustine likewise transformed an insight originating in Stoicism concerning the temporal relations of images. While Platonists and Aristotelians focused on the transitoriness of images, Stoics argued that every image reflects two dimensions of time, namely past and present. Augustine proposed that this two-sidedness is principally a feature of memory images, since these are the types of images that are most easily recognized by the mind as belonging to the past but are universally experienced in the present. Augustine limited his discussion of this aspect of images to problems of recall, especially in the *Confessions*, book 10, and in *De Trinitate*, and did not apply this insight to poetic images. This step was taken by Petrarch, who argued against the position of "Augustinus" in the *Secretum* and advocated the view that it is through images, and images alone, that the temporal nature of ethical thinking can be adequately expressed by means of poetry. Petrarch thus suggested that poetry and philosophy are different ways of approaching the same moral issues.

One of the lessons of the *Confessions* is that each of us has an ethical responsibility for our memories. In Augustine's approach to self-knowledge, "the remembrance of things past" replaces the Socratic dialogue as the starting point for achieving virtue. In book 10 of his autobiography Augustine combs his memory for different sorts of images that can be used in the mental recovery of the self's narrative. He is convinced that personal identity is largely constructed by means of such memories, and that as a consequence "self" and "memory" are interdependent concepts.[31] In the end he dismisses impressions as a guide to truth or falsehood. But he does not replace them with Platonic forms: instead, he adopts a combination of the Aristotelian/Stoic views, in which sense impressions play a large role in the acquisition of knowledge, and the Neoplatonic view, according to which the veracity of such impressions can only be judged by the mind.

Augustine's writings on memory contain a good many thought experiments whose purpose is to study the mental record of events, not according to abstract definitions, but as a consequence of what we see, hear, and remember. His experimental attitude in turn influences his interpretive methods for dealing with memories. In the process of this introspective thinking he liberally substitutes one sort of memory image for another, intermingling images derived from sense perceptions with those drawn from his literary and biblical studies. He thereby introduces a new dimension to the study of the literary imagination: the notion of a valid but second-order level of literary experience in which, to use his own terminology, *phantasiae* and *phantasmata* have roughly equal status. The created universe, he notes, impresses us with its visual beauty no less than God's rhetorical presentation of the act of creation in the Bible.[32]

Augustine also has important insights on the relation between memory and emotion. Just as Aristotle separates sense perceptions and judgments about them, Augustine separates sense perceptions and the emotions that may subsequently arise from these impressions. The critical text on the subject is book 3, chapter 2, of the *Confessions*, where he engages in a Platonically inspired criticism of drama. As noted in my first lecture, he asks why something that is false, namely a fictional performance, can give rise to emotions that are genuinely felt. The source of these emotions is a mere representation; yet in contrast to Plato he observes that emotions have the same truth for the person who experiences them, whether their source is false or true. Elsewhere he argues that we have the identical fear when confronted by a genuine criminal as we do when we meet a passerby whom we think intends us harm.[33]

Our emotions are real, therefore, even though their source may be unreal: this view reverses a Platonic axiom stating that where the source is false, the emotion will of necessity be inauthentic. Augustine argues further that reason, by which Plato distinguishes true and false emotions, can never succeed in its task, because, in the equation between reason and emotion, it is often emotion that is the constant and reason the variable. This is one of the lessons of the narrative books of the *Confessions*, which relate a series of emotional challenges that Augustine faces and carefully chart his failures to deal with them by means of reason. But if his emotions are true in this sense, they are special kinds of truths, which he admits that he never fully understands.

As a consequence, he knows that he cannot rely on himself alone if he wishes to achieve the stability and equilibrium sought by ancient thinkers, in which emotion is kept under control. He has to be assisted by a force superior to human reason, which can transcend the limitations that he believes he has inherited through original sin. His realization of his weakness with respect to emotion is one of the mainsprings of his doctrine of grace and the source of his abandonment of rational philosophy in favor of religion.

In addition to reversing some accepted views on emotions, Augustine links emotional memories to the experience of time. On this theme his thinking is in harmony with that of Plato. As mentioned, he drew from Plato the notion of man as an artist, who imitates the creative activity of God. The source of his views is *Timaeus* 27d (and following), where Plato utilizes the three distinctions subsequently found in Augustine's treatment of memory to describe the eternal and temporal worlds. The unchanging world is grasped through the intellect, which corresponds to Augustine's images of number and dimension, whereas the changing world is only a "likeness" of the changeless world, on which it is modeled: this corresponds to Augustine's other types of memory images, *phantasiae* and *phantasmata*. Where he goes beyond Plato in his approach to memory is in proposing that this threefold structure is a part of both human psychology and the historical development of civilization. It is by analogy with the concepts of eternity and time in the *Timaeus* that he patterns his conception of the eternal and temporal cities in *De Civitate Dei*: "the two cities, the earthly and the heavenly . . . which we find . . . interwoven, as it were, in this present transitory world, and mingled with one another."[34]

3

Augustine marks the high point of late ancient thinking about memory images and the ethics of reading. In the remainder of this lecture I would like to provide some illustrations of the ways in which this subject is transformed by two medieval and two nineteenth-century writers.

I turn first to Dante and Petrarch, who died respectively in 1321 and 1374. The text of Dante that I wish to discuss briefly is the opening scene of the *Vita Nuova*, which was written between 1292 and 1294. The subject of this work is Dante's youthful love for Beatrice Portinari, whom the poet first saw in 1274, when they were both nine years old. The *Vita* charts the progress of the author's emotions down to her death and during his life afterward. In the opening two chapters the themes of reading, memory, and imagination are introduced in a manner that both recalls and transcends the Augustinian synthesis. "In that part of the book of my memory" (*libro de la mia memoria*), Dante states, "where previously there would be little to read" (*poco . . . leggere*) "is found a rubric which says: *Incipit vita nova*" (The incipit or title is "New Life"). "Under that heading," he adds, "I find written the words that it is my intention to bring together in this book, at least as regards their significance" (*almeno la loro sentenzia*).[35]

Dante subsequently "reads" in the book of his personal memory, just as Augustine reads the Bible in the *Confessions*; but whereas the maxims that Augustine draws from this reading are not a part of his autobiography, Dante finds the text of words he himself and others have spoken (*io trovo scritte le parole . . .*), whose meaning he plans to summarize. And while Augustine downplays poetry and *phantasia*, Dante emphasizes the role that emotion and imagination play in his first sighting of Beatrice, stating: "I say that from that time [the god of] Love was the master of my soul . . . over which he ruled with such assurance and dominion through the force that is given to my imagination" (*per la vertù che li dava la mia imaginazione*) "that I agreed to attend completely to his every pleasure."

It is God who rules Augustine's soul, but Love that rules Dante's. Augustine distrusts sensory images, as potential sources of error and unwanted feelings, whereas Dante finds their emotional import significant, at times overwhelming.[36] Augustine's sole true love is for God, and he finds the wisdom that results from that commitment in the Bible; Dante's love is both for God and for a woman, and, as a layman, he finds the sources of wisdom both in the Bible and in the civic institutions that Aristotle viewed as the foundation of ethics in lay society. As a consequence of this modification, physical pleasures (*piaceri*) are not ascetically refused: they are aesthetically transformed. Finally, no less in Dante than in Augustine, this manner of dealing with emotions is a readerly affair. Dante comments on his poems, just as Augustine comments on the Bible; he presents his lyrics as objects of sensory beauty, then outlines their significance for his spiritual progress.

By contrast, in Petrarch's *rime* the combination of lyric expression and personal commentary is built into the poems themselves. My example of this phenomenon is taken from *Canzoniere* 3.[37] The subject of the sonnet is Petrarch's first sighting of Laura, which took place on 6 April 1327:

> Era il giorno ch'al sol si scoloraro
> per la pietà del suo factore i rai
> quando i' fui preso, et non me ne guardai,
> ché i be' vostr' occhi, donna, mi legaro.

Tempo non mi parea da far riparo
contra colpi d'Amor: però m'andai
secur, senza sospetto; onde i miei guai
nel commune dolor s'incominciaro.

Trovommi Amor del tutto disarmato
et aperta la via per gli occhi al core,
che di lagrime son fatti uscio et varco:

però al mio parer non li fu honore
ferir me de saetta in quello stato,
a voi armata non mostrar pur l'arco.

[It was the day when the sun's rays turned pale with grief
for his Maker when I was taken, and I did not defend
   myself
against it, for your lovely eyes, Lady, bound me.

It did not seem to me a time for being on guard against
Love's blows; therefore I went confident and without
   fear,
and so my misfortunes began in the midst of the
   universal woe.

Love found me altogether disarmed, and the way
open through my eyes to my heart, my eyes which are
now the portal and passageway of tears.

Therefore, as it seems to me, it got him no honour
to strike me with an arrow in that state, and not even to
show his bow to you, who were armed.]

The topic of this poem is the same as that of the opening
chapter of the *Vita Nuova*, with which Petrarch was well acquainted. This is the sighting of the loved one by her potential lover: the piercing glance, by which, in Provençal and
earlier Italian lyric, love's arrow enters the lover's heart and
enslaves his emotions. In poem 3 the event takes place at
Easter: the memory of the crucifixion, to which Petrarch
refers as "universal woe," coincides with the appearance of

his idealized Laura on earth. Dante uses Augustine's notion of a "book of memory" as his point of departure, but the *Vita Nuova* is not truly Augustinian in form; it is written as a *satura*, a mixture of prose and verse, along the model of Boethius's *Consolation of Philosophy*. By contrast, Petrarch returns to Augustine's method of contrasting different periods of his life within a single narrative. It is this technique that gives the lyrics of the *Canzoniere* their moral thrust as well as their unity within his spiritual autobiography. In book 11 of *The City of God*, Augustine speaks of collecting "the scattered traces of [God's] being in the world" (11.28). Petrarch speaks of his "song-book" as *Rerum Vulgarium Fragmenta*: this too is a collection of fragments, but refers to his life rather than to God's creation. The *Canzoniere* is an attempt through memory to overcome the fragmentation of the self; as Augustine says, possibly with Plotinus in mind, at *Confessions* 2.1.1: *colligens me a dispersione*. Whereas Dante is straightforward in his reaction to the appearance of his beloved in the *Vita Nuova*, recording the visual effects of Beatrice's appearance, Petrarch is detached, even somewhat ironic when thinking of Laura: his sun is pale, his defeat is unanticipated, and his happiness arises from his tears.

Dante and Petrarch thus invite comparison with Romantic writers. They are distant forerunners of the conception of the imagination in Wordsworth and Coleridge, the one based on association and excitement, the other on creative rewriting and philosophical distance. And they differ from Plato and Augustine in their approach to mimesis: Plato relies on reason to judge the truthfulness of images, and Augustine on God, whereas the medieval authors ask above all for the arbitration of the reader.

. . .

To summarize: I began this lecture with the problem of falsity and truth in literature, suggesting that a part of the story is incorporated into the history of the word *phantasia*. Aristotle questions Plato's association between *phantasia* and judgment, while Augustine questions the link between *phantasia* and emotion. Aristotle and Augustine agree that *phantasiai* are often mistaken, while perceptions are not: for Aristotle, therefore, a false *phantasia* can give rise to a true judgment, while, for Augustine, a false *phantasia* can give rise to a true emotion.

Twelfth-century authors widen the range of situations in which it is possible to distinguish between the falsity of a sensory source and the truth of a resulting emotional experience. In doing so, they anticipate Coleridge's dictum on poets as philosophers. Augustine, in writing the *Confessions*, pictures himself as an outsider to God's unity and harmoniousness, and can only read about these aspects of the divine story in the Bible. By contrast, later allegorical poets such as Bernard Silvester, Alan of Lille, Guillaume de Lorris, and Jean de Meun combine Plato's notion of innate ideas and the biblical narrative of creation, thus providing a mental stage on which the reflective or meditative reader can observe the drama of the creative imagination from within. As in Plato, this is a drama of both being and becoming, but one in which the principal parts are no longer played by philosophical abstractions but by human emotions.

In Dante and Petrarch, who are the successors to the philosophical poets of the twelfth century, another boundary separating ancient from early modern thinking on the ethics of reading is crossed. These authors agree with Augustine that the emotions generated by literature are genuine. But they add a detail that would not have been accepted by the bishop of Hippo, namely that the secular literature of love, in particular lyric poetry, can give rise to virtuous emotions. In their writing love poetry takes its place alongside epic, tragic drama, and scripture as a source of moral conduct and as a means of talking about it, preparing the way for the Renaissance artistic combination of *mimesis* and *phantasia*.[38] This is a double challenge to ancient views—the suggestion that images matter and that those concerned with love may matter most.

To conclude this section of the discussion, I note briefly the confirmation of the imagination's role in ethics in the *De Imaginatione* of Gianfrancesco Pico della Mirandola (d. 1553),[39] which is typical of Renaissance syntheses on the theme and looks forward to the more optimistic *Defence of Poesy* by Sir Philip Sidney, written two generations later. Gianfrancesco agrees with Aristotle that the imagination can be influenced negatively by illness, lack of sleep, or other psychological factors, but argues that "our actions for the most part depend on the inventiveness of this power," within which is understood "the entire force of that aspect of the soul that is oriented for or by the senses."[40] He concludes that God gave man imagination as a part of his design in order to enhance relations between body and soul:

What communication would the rational part have with the irrational, if there were not phantasy intermediate [*phantasia intermedia*], somehow to prepare for reason the inferior nature. For when the imagination has received the impressions of objects from the senses, it retains them within itself, and, having rendered them more pure, offers them to the active intellect."[41]

Yet the ascetic impulse has to dominate the aesthetic:

Since the life of man is slippery, and inclined to blundering and failure, and, as Holy Writ reminds us, is from early youth prone to evil, . . . what we ought to use for our happiness we abuse for our

misery and unhappiness. Were we to proceed with the light native
to us as our guide, we should accumulate no evil from the faults
of phantasy . . . , seeing that we should by sway of reason rule over
phantasy, and not follow it; we should suppress phantasy, if it errs,
and not urge it on. He who strives to dominate phantasy persists
in that dignity in which he was created and placed. . . .[42]

In chapters 6 to 10, Gianfrancesco describes the harm done
to statecraft and the pursuit of the philosophical life by unbridled fantasies and provides an explanation for the errors
of fantasies according to the medieval doctrine of the hu-
mors and emotions. He stresses the role played by free will
in overcoming their baleful influence.

4

Two thinkers who benefited from the Renaissance reevaluation of the imagination were Samuel Taylor Coleridge
(d. 1834) and Arthur Schopenhauer (d. 1860), with whom I
would like to conclude.

It is widely acknowledged that the pair develop in different directions out of Kant's theory of aesthetic judgments, in
particular from *The Critique of Judgement*, where the topics of the formal purposefulness of nature and the creative
freedom of the artist are discussed. Like Kant, they are convinced that critical theory in the arts and literature should
form part of a general philosophy in which there is an organic and even architectonic relationship between parts and
whole. To this venerable notion they add the view that criticism, in particular criticism of literature, has to adopt the
methods of philosophy rather than limit itself to description, classification, or treatment of technical matters. As in
Kant, but differently from Kant, therefore, in their writings

criticism is concerned with categories of thought and with their accompanying theoretical structures.

Coleridge and Schopenhauer likewise share with other Romantic writers an interest in consciousness, the creative imagination, and inspirational "genius." They have a transcendental view of art and literature, which is loosely based on Platonist thinking. Coleridge incorporates this doctrine into a metaphysical position indebted to Christianity, whereas Schopenhauer rules out metaphysics, despite the indirect influence of metaphysical thinking on his concept of the will. If Coleridge creatively misunderstands Kant,[43] whose views he intermingles with those of Schelling, Schopenhauer errs in another direction in attempting to reconstitute Kant's authentic doctrines against the background of what he believes to be misinterpretations on the part of Hegel and Fichte. Notwithstanding these divergencies, the positions of Coleridge and Schopenhauer can both be traced to Leibniz's observation to the effect that aesthetic judgments by mortals are not absolute but relative and inevitably concern the subjective evaluation of one work of art against another. In this respect, their views anticipate the contemporary concern with critical relativism and audience response in determining the ethical parameters of literature and art.

Coleridge's views on the imagination developed in stages throughout his writings; however, the well-known synthesis of his thinking on the subject occurs in chapter 13 of *Biographia Literaria*, a work written in 1815 and published in 1817, where he makes the following distinctions:

The IMAGINATION then I consider either as primary, or secondary. The primary imagination I hold to be the living Power and prime Agent of all human Perception, and as a repetition in the finite mind of the eternal act of creation in the infinite I AM. The secondary I consider as an echo of the former, co-existing with the conscious will, yet still as identical with the primary in the *kind* of its agency, and differing only in *degree*, and in the *mode* of its operation. It dissolves, diffuses, dissipates, in order to re-create; or where this process is rendered impossible, yet still at all events it struggles to idealize and to unify. It is essentially *vital*, even as all objects (*as* objects) are essentially fixed and dead.

FANCY, on the contrary, has no other counters to play with, but fixities and definites. The Fancy is indeed no other than a mode of Memory emancipated from the order of time and space; and blended with, and modified by that empirical phenomenon of the will, which we express by the word CHOICE. But equally with the ordinary memory it must receive all its materials ready made from the law of association.[44]

In this statement, which has been characterized as "one of the most famous passages in all of English prose and one the least satisfactorily understood,"[45] Coleridge is chiefly reacting against the conception of the mind as a *tabula rasa*, which had been advanced by Hobbes, Locke, Hume, and Hartley. On this view, which was summed up by Samuel Johnson in his *Dictionary of the English Language* in 1775, imagination was defined, as noted earlier, as "fancy: the power of forming ideal pictures; the power of representing things absent to oneself or others." Many eighteenth-century English thinkers were convinced that imagination was a function of memory and either reproduced sense perceptions based on experience or brought together perceptions not based on experience. By contrast, Coleridge proposes the distinction, based on Schelling's *Einbildungskraft* and *Phantasie* (which in turn depend on Kant's *produktiv* and *reproductiv* in the first edition of the *Kritik der praktischen Vernunft*), between imagination, linked to reason, and fancy, linked to understanding.[46] Through an eclectic reading of these sources, Coleridge became convinced that imagination is an active and creative power in the mind, often working independently of external or environmental influences; therefore, it is not a faculty for recording or rearranging sense impressions held in memory, but a shaping instrument, guided by the will, which modifies the givens of experience under the influence of inner enlightenment or illumination.

The mind, then, as Wordsworth noted, is "a balance, an ennobling interchange/Of action from within and from without,"[47] possessing what Coleridge calls the "esemplastic" power "to shape into one" its many and varied constituents.[48] The conception of a passive receptacle is rejected: in its place, Coleridge speaks of the work of the imagination, which includes sense, perception, memory, emotion, and intellect, all bound together by poetic language. In the shaping of this viewpoint he was stimulated by the writings of the Neoplatonist and pantheist Ralph Cudworth, whose *True Intellectual System* he annotated in 1795, as well as by philosophical and scientific works that he read in Germany from 1798 to 1799. He eventually disagreed with Wordsworth's claim in the 1800 preface to *Lyrical Ballads* that poetry results from "the manner in which we associate ideas in a state of excitement," and proposed instead a combination of reflections on past and present, thought and feeling, involving a large creative role for the imagination.

Among his sources are Plotinus[49] (who entered English thinking via Thomas Taylor), from whom he may have acquired one of the principles guiding his psychological outlook. This is the view that the mind derives much knowledge from sense perceptions but not its awareness of itself and its inherent forms of consciousness, which are generated within.[50] A supporting influence is Leibniz, quoted at the beginning of chapter 13, who argues that the mind, in comprehending what is around it, acts like a mirror for reality. Coleridge extended these notions to include the human reflection of the infinite mind of God. The result is a threefold division of imagination, paralleling will, the soul's immortality, and God's existence, which is trintarian in form.

Another formative influence was Johann Nicolaus Tetens (1736–1807), whose *Philosophische Versuche über die menschliche Natur und ihre Entwickelung* of 1775–1776 divided imagination into *Perceptionsvermögen*, *Phantasie*, and *Dichtungskraft*, thus paralleling Coleridge's threefold division of imagination into notions of primary and secondary imagination and fancy.[51] Tetens wrote that the act of representation

> can be conceived under three headings. First we produce original representations out of the sensations within us. . . . This is perception. . . . Secondly, this power of sensation is reproduced even when those first sensations have ceased. . . . This effect is commonly ascribed to the . . . fancy.
>
> *Thirdly.* This reproduction of the ideas is still not all, however, that the human power of representation does with them. It does not merely reproduce them, it does not merely alter their previous coexistence . . . but also creates new images and representations. . . . The soul is able not only to arrange and order its representations, like the curator of a gallery of paintings, but is itself a painter, and invents and constructs new paintings.
>
> These achievements belong to the *Dichtungsvermögen*, a creative power, whose sphere of activity seems to have a great scope. . . . It is the self-active fancy . . . and without doubt an essential ingredient of genius.[52]

Tetens, an influence on Kant, may well be echoing the *Philebus* in his reference to the analogy between imagination and painting; he is also indebted to Alexander Gerard, whose *Essay on Genius* appeared in 1774, and Christian Wolff, whose *Psychologia empirica* and *Psychologia rationalis* were published respectively in 1732 and 1734. "What was happening," note the editors of the *Biographia Literaria*, "was that philosophers were expanding the rôle of the imagination. . . . As the eighteenth century progressed, the imagination was keeping its elementary slot in faculty psychology between the senses and the understanding, but was also being credited with artistic creativity."[53] This sounds like a return to the psychological and philosophical interest in mental images that characterized antiquity and late antiquity, and in some ways it was. The two sides of this discussion were represented in England by Locke and Berkeley on the one hand and by figures like Addison and Akenside on the other hand, the latter's study, *The Pleasures of the Imagination*, appearing in 1744.[54] Like their ancient predecessors, Tetens and Coleridge engaged in studies that attempted to connect science and poetry, assuming that the one could explain the other.

Coleridge shared with Wordsworth the view that progress through the three levels of imagination is not only intellectual and artistic but also moral, even theological.[55] He thus found himself on common ground with ancient, late ancient, and medieval thinkers for whom there is no separation between secular and religious approaches to the imagination or between reading and writing as interconnected meditative activities.[56] In both epochs creation begins with perception: the mind, operating subjectively, transforms objective stimuli, and makes wholes out of parts, order out of chaos. He was equally convinced, as were many patristic thinkers, that Plato had prepared the way for Christianity[57] by means of the implementation of an ascetic methodology

and the practice of spiritual exercises: "Plato began in meditation, thought deeply within himself of the goings-on of
his own mind . . . and then looked abroad to ask if this were
a dream, or whether it were indeed a revelation from within.
. . . He employed his observation as the interpreter of his
meditation."[58]

Early Christian thinkers, whom Coleridge equally reinterpreted, did not believe that the individual's inner resources are most fully expressed in the poetic imagination:
they nonetheless anticipated his view that it is free will, as
an aspect of mind or self, that guides creative and charitable
literary activity, and that this guidance comes from within
the heart. Commentators viewed the Bible as a divinely inspired combination of rhetoric and philosophy, therefore
superior to the worldly creations of either Vergil or Plato.
In late ancient Christians and in Coleridge, therefore, the
human creativity involved in writing or reading acquired a
moral and metaphysical dimension.[59] This was a response to
Plato's view in the *Republic*: through the imagination, philosophy is poetry, poetry philosophy.[60]

The question is how these views entered Coleridge's
thinking. Did he absorb them via German thinkers who
were already indebted to a variety of "Platonisms"? Or did
he base his notion on the originals, such as Johannes Scottus
Eriugena, the early medieval synthesizer of Greek and Latin
Platonism whose *Periphyseon* he scrupulously annotated,
believing the ninth-century author a pantheist and the fore-
runner of his beloved Spinoza?[61] On the one hand, it is possible, as M. H. Abrams proposed, that "through his early
readings in Platonists and mystics, Coleridge had acquired
the essentials of his idealism prior to his first knowledge of
German philosophy";[62] on the other hand, Thomas McFarland has stated authoritatively that there is "no convinc-

ing context" that "the viewpoints of Kant and other German thinkers could have found their way into Coleridge's thought from Platonist sources."[63]

In discussing these issues a distinction has to be made between Plato and his successors, many of whom did not hold authentically Platonist views. In fact, if the term "Platonist" in the *Biographia* is taken to refer to the statements of Plato himself, both the claim of a primordial Platonic influence and the attempted rebuttal of that thesis are somewhat off track. What Coleridge associated with Platonist aesthetics was based on Plato's theory of forms but had little to do with the views on poetry, painting, and the other mimetic arts stated in books 1, 3, and 10 of the *Republic*, which, taken together, provide a summary of his thinking on the ethics of reading epic poetry. Coleridge's Platonism was a synthesis of Plato, Plotinus,[64] and later contributions, including those of the Cambridge Platonists. The only clear distinction that he made between Plato and Plotinus was on the question of pantheism: there he relied on his misreadings of Plotinus and Eriugena supported by selective quotations from Schelling. His Platonism was therefore an intellectual construct largely of his own invention, and subsumed under its rubric much that came from other sources on ascetic themes. He himself suggests as much in *Table Talk*, 30 April 1830, where he remarks that "Plato's works are preparatory exercises for the mind. . . . I have read most of the works of Plato several times with profound attention, but not all his writings. In fact, I soon found that I had read Plato by anticipation."

The neglect of this problem has implications for our understanding of the celebrated statement on "fancy" and "imagination." What is striking in Coleridge's definitions is not the distinction, which is made in one way or another by many ancient students of *phantasia*, but the demarcation between nontemporal and temporal factors in consciousness. Primary imagination, as it is envisaged by Coleridge, is a temporal "repetition" of a nontemporal force, just as Plato's time is the "moving image" of eternity. However Coleridge's nontemporal force is not Plato's demiurge but the Judeo-Christian God, "I am who am." In this respect, Coleridge reflects Plato's distinction as it is reformulated by patristic thinkers, for whom the proof of self-existence is the proof of the presence within man of the image of the eternal deity. Coleridge senses, although he is evidently not quoting, Augustine's view that the test for the existence of the self or soul, later known as the Cartesian *cogito*, is a mental and spiritual exercise by which man's reason progresses upward toward a partial understanding of a deity whom he can never fully know.

Coleridge reverses the priorities in the ancient relationship between ascetic and aesthetic criticism, suggesting that the former can be an outgrowth of the latter. The comparable figure on the Continent is Arthur Schopenhauer, who approaches the relevant questions in a more strictly philosophical fashion.

The theme of reading appears in the 1818 edition of *The World as Will and Idea*, where it functions, not as a framework for a conception of the imagination, as in Coleridge, but in the first instance as an illustrative metaphor within a discussion of life and dreams. Supported by texts of philosophy (Kant), mythology (Vedas, Puranas), and literature (Pindar, Sophocles, Calderón, Shakespeare), Schopenhauer sums up his thinking by means of a quotation from Shakespeare's *Tempest*, act 4, scene 1:

> We are such stuff
> As dreams are made on, and our little life
> Is rounded with a sleep.

He then comments:[65]

After the numerous quotations from the poets, perhaps I also may be allowed to express myself by a metaphor. Life and dreams are leaves of the same book. The systematic reading of this book is real life, but when the reading hours (that is, the day) are over, we often continue idly to turn over the leaves, and read a page here and there without method or connection: often one we have read before, sometimes one that is new to us, but always in the same book. Such an isolated page is indeed out of connection with the systematic study of the book, but it does not seem so very different when we remember that the whole continuous perusal begins and ends just as abruptly, and may therefore be regarded as merely a larger single page.

In Schopenhauer's view, then, life is a kind of dream, and, as a result, dreams are a kind of life. We are aware that these versions of narrative differ, since, when we awaken from a dream, we know we have been dreaming. Yet, as a type of *mimesis*, dreams operate within life as an alternative form of continuity and, like lived experience, create within the mind a sensation of duration. Like many medieval thinkers, Schopenhauer finds it convenient to see life as an all-encompassing book, in which the pages are somehow "read"; and, in a Petrarchan moment, he thinks of the individual "leaves" as self-contained episodes, each with its own story to tell. Further, in describing waking and dreaming, he distinguishes between images arising from "systematic reading," which are experienced at the time of the reading, and those arising from the mental perusal of the book's "leaves," the latter of which are derived from subject's thoughts about the text after it has been read. This is a version of "recollected experience."

Yet, in speaking about memories, he differs from Wordsworth and Coleridge in one respect. He is convinced that by examining the reading process important aspects of consciousness can be revealed without the necessity of traditional metaphysical assumptions.[66] His rejection takes the form of a declaration of autonomy for the reading process as an affair of human communication alone. Emphasis is placed on the phenomena of time—on duration and internal time-consciousness—but without the suggestion that these notions are connected to any larger framework beyond the person. "Inwardly in self-consciousness," he notes perceptively, "I know myself in *time* alone."[67] Elsewhere he observes that time "is something residing within us, our own mental process advancing uninterruptedly. . . . The uniformity and regularity of its course in all heads shows more than anything else that it is one being or entity that dreams it."[68]

In the first quoted passage, then, reading is a way of talking about consciousness, just as consciousness is a way of talking about reading. Both processes are symbolized by the "leaves" of a book, which are read differently in living and dreaming. But what precisely is meant by these terms, life and dreams? The "life" that Schopenhauer has in mind is not passive, unthinking existence, which he, like ancient thinkers, associates with lower animals, but a time of reflection, self-consciousness, and personal examination. Within this *bios* a large part of one's reflections takes place on what one has read—philosophy, mythology, and literature. Lived experience is interdependent with our interpretation of that experience. We are what we read: we read to become what we are. And in harmony with this view, a dream is considered a product of the creative imagination.

The question Schopenhauer asks in his preface is not so different from the one proposed by Plato, Augustine, Dante, and Montaigne: this concerns the intellectual status of *phantasiae* and their ethical value. On this topic he takes an uncompromising ascetic position, stating that

> in all that concerns our weal and woe, we should *keep a tight reign on our imagination.* . . . Our imagination . . . builds bright castles in the air in quite a leisurely fashion. . . . Therefore, things that affect our weal and woe should be considered by us with reason and judgement and consequently with cool and dispassionate deliberation. Imagination should be left out of the question, for it is not competent to judge. On the contrary, it conjures up mere images or pictures that agitate our feelings unprofitably. . . . If the objects of our meditation concern our personal affairs, they can then easily . . . become terrifying pictures.[69]

Proof of this point is found in the deployment of the literary texts that precede the first quoted passage. Attention is not drawn to their aesthetic qualities—to the beauty of the metaphors, the music of the verse, or the artistic settings—but to their relevance to the question under discussion, namely the dreamlike quality of life. Shakespeare's lines from *The Tempest* act as a supporting text for this endeavor rather than as a metaphorical statement in a dramatic work, even though elsewhere Schopenhauer expresses his admiration for the purely aesthetic qualities of literature and art, for example, in his correspondence with Goethe before 1814.

This ascetic project differs from the comparable schemes in Plato or Augustine, both of whom he admired.[70] Plato measures the moral effectiveness of literature against the claims of reason and Augustine against the claims of faith, whereas Schopenhauer limits himself to a contrast between "systematic" reading, which follows the logic of the text, and mental rereading, which takes place "without method or connection." Speech, which is the source of Plato's *logos* and Augustine's *Verbum Dei*, is viewed as a transparent medium of communication and a receptacle for thought, as distinct from imagination (I, 50):

> Speech, as an object of outer experience, is obviously nothing more than a very complete telegraph, which communicates arbitrary signs with the greatest rapidity and the finest distinctions of differences. But what do these signs mean? How are they interpreted? When someone speaks, do we at once translate his words into pictures of the fancy . . . ? What a tumult there would be in our brains while we listened to a speech, or to the reading of a book! But what actually happens is not this at all. The meaning of a speech is, as a rule, immediately grasped, . . . without the imagination being brought into play. It is reason which speaks to reason, keeping within its province. It communicates and receives abstract conceptions, ideas that cannot be presented in perceptions, which are framed once for all, and relatively few in number, but which yet encompass, contain, and represent all the innumerable objects of the actual world.

Schopenhauer's is a traditional type of asceticism, reminiscent of Seneca, in which the reader, assuming that the text conveys accurate information, subjects postreading imaginative "fancy" to a mental discipline inspired by reading. Elsewhere he illustrates the manner in which such concepts overlap in the mind through the analogy of traveling (*peregrinari*, I, 64f.).[71] Concepts have permanence, like written texts, but this rigidity is their chief limitation: they are "stones of a mosaic, of which perceptions always remain their asymptote. . . . Nothing good is produced in art by their means" (I, 74). As a consequence, "virtue and holiness do not proceed from reflection," which arises from concepts or reason, but "from the inner depths of the will" (I, 75). A man (or woman) lives two lives, one in the "concrete," the other in the "abstract" (I, 112):

In the former he is given as prey to all the storms of actual life, and to the influence of the present. . . . But his life in the abstract, as it lies before his rational consciousness, is the still reflection of the former, and of the world in which he lives. . . . Here in the sphere of quiet deliberation, what completely possessed him and moved him intensely before, appears to him cold, colourless, and for the moment external to him; he is merely the spectator, the observer. In respect of this withdrawal into reflection he may be compared to an actor who has played his part in one scene, and who takes his place among the audience till it is time for him to go upon the stage again, and quietly looks on at whatever may happen. . . .

Schopenhauer likewise proposes that "genius" consists "in the capacity for knowing, independently of the principle of sufficient reason, not individual things, which have their existence only in their relations, but [on the contrary consists] in the Ideas of such things, and of being oneself the correlative of this Idea, and thus no longer an individual, but the pure subject of knowledge." This capacity exists to some degree in every person (although, he grants, largely unrealized) as an innate "power of knowing the Ideas in things, and consequently of transcending their personality for the moment," thus constituting a type of meditative withdrawal. As a consequence of this universally shared ability, he argues that "the man of genius excels ordinary men only by possessing this kind of knowledge in a far higher degree and more continuously." He has a parallel explanation for the appreciative reception of works of art, in which "this Idea [perceived to be in things] remains unchanged and the same, so that aesthetic pleasure is one and the same whether it is called forth by a work of art or directly by the contemplation of nature and life." As a result, "the work of art is only a means of facilitating the knowledge in which this pleasure consists" (III, 251–252).

The manner in which this higher perception is realized is

by abandoning practical, sufficient, and instrumental forms of reasoning in favor of a contemplative mode of thought; this proceeds in Platonic fashion from outer phenomenal appearances to inner forms that are not perceptible by means of the senses. The will then comes into focus as the central impediment to creativity: "In the aesthetical mode of contemplation we have found *two inseparable constituent parts* — the knowledge of the object, not as individual thing but as Platonic Idea, that is, as the enduring form of this whole species of things; and the self-consciousness of the knowing person, not as individual, but as *pure will-less subject of knowledge. . . .*" In order to achieve artistic insights, therefore, it is necessary to overcome willing, which "arises . . . from deficiency, and therefore from suffering," fixing the individual and his or her desires within the bounds of time (III, 253–254):

But when some external cause or inward disposition lifts us suddenly out of the endless stream of willing, delivers knowledge from the slavery of the will, the attention is no longer directed to the motives of the willing, but comprehends things from their relation to the will. . . . Then all at once the peace which we were always seeking, but which always fled from us on the former path of the desires, comes to us of its own accord, and it is well with us. . . .

But this is just the state which I described above as necessary for the knowledge of the Idea, as pure contemplation, as sinking oneself in perception, losing oneself in the object, forgetting all individuality, surrendering that kind of knowledge which follows the principles of sufficient reason, and comprehends only relations.

This is a clearly meditative state: an "inward disposition," in which there is a "predominance of knowing over willing," even though it is a frame of mind brought about "by the inner power of an artistic nature" (III, 253).

The pathway by which the individual attains this level of interiority is not outlined in detail by Schopenhauer, who prefers to talk about the poles of willing and knowing rather than the steps that lead the person of artistic temperament from one to the other (III, 256): "For at the moment at which, freed from the will, we give ourselves up to pure will-less knowing, we pass into a world from which everything is absent that influenced our will and moved us so violently through it. This freeing of knowledge lifts us as wholly and entirely from all that, as do sleep and dreams; happiness and unhappiness have disappeared; we are no longer individual; the individual is forgotten; we are the only pure subject of knowledge. . . ."

In these statements Schopenhauer combines ascetic and aesthetic orientations in a manner in which, as in Coleridge, the latter appear to be derivable from, if not dependent upon, the former. The attempt to link these notions forms part of his response to the rationalist methodologies of Descartes, Spinoza, and Leibniz, which he frequently attacks both through arguments and through his conviction concerning the possible ascent of the mind from perceptible to nonperceptible realms. As Patrick Gardiner observes, this demonstration does not imply

any irrationalist consequences; essentially, it represents the standpoint adopted before Schopenhauer by both Hume and Kant. . . . He insisted, for instance . . . despite everything that had been said in the *Critique of Pure Reason*, [that] German philosophers were once more writing as if they had mysterious access to a type of knowledge that Kant had shown to be in principle impossible, deriving from "a wholly imaginary, fictitious faculty."[72]

Given these presuppositions, Schopenhauer's manner of approaching philosophical problems has a great deal in common with that of Montaigne: he does not think of philosophy in terms of "demonstrations," nor does he proceed deductively. There is no beginning and end to his reflections; no attempt is made to summarize or synthesize his views on the various topics on which he touches. Above all, his mode of thought is not cumulative but ruminative and reiterative—almost, at times, a kind of thinking and speaking memory. On this view philosophy is not a linear, upward chain of reasoning but should be "conceived as a pendulum swinging between *rationalism* and *illuminism*."[73]

He says as much in different words in the preface to the 1818 edition of *The World as Will and Idea*. After advising his readers to become familiar with his Western and Eastern sources,[74] as well as his little-noticed doctoral dissertation on the fourfold source of sufficient reason, he tells them (p. vii) "how this book must be read in order to be thoroughly understood. By means of it I only intend to impart a single thought. Yet, notwithstanding all my endeavours, I could find no shorter way of imparting it than this whole book. I hold this thought to be that which has very long been sought for under the name of philosophy. . . . [which] exhibits itself as that which we call metaphysics, . . . ethics, . . . and aesthetics." He subsequently contrasts "a system of thought," which requires "an architectonic connection or coherence," and "a single thought," which, no matter how "comprehensive," has to "preserve . . . unity" in a manner in which the parts support the whole and vice versa. In systematic thinking unity comes about by means of the organization of the text, whereas an "organic" presentation is in large part determined by the reader's imitation of the contemplative practice that has gone into the work's composition. To "enter into the thought . . . in the work," therefore, the book has to be read *twice* (pp. viii–ix): "the first time with great patience, a patience which is only to be derived from the belief, voluntarily accorded, that the beginning presupposes the end almost as much as the end presupposes the beginning . . . , after which, on a second perusal, much, or all, will appear in an entirely different light." Furthermore, "the structure of the whole, which is organic, not a mere chain, makes it necessary sometimes to touch upon the same point twice. . . . This construction . . . [is not by means of] chapters and paragraphs . . . [but] four principal divisions, as it were four aspects of one thought."

Schopenhauer generalizes this position in relation to other thinkers like himself in a later essay, noting that "the real thinkers had aimed at *insight*, and indeed for its own sake, since they ardently desired in some way to render comprehensible the world in which they happened to be; but this they did not do in order to teach and talk. And so, in consequence of constant meditation, there gradually grows in them a fixed, coherent, and fundamental view which always has as its basis the apprehension of the world through *intuitive perception*."[75] He acknowledges the contributions of both the conscious and unconscious in framing and solving problems: "We might almost imagine that half of all our thinking occurred unconsciously. The conclusion is in most cases drawn without the premises having been clearly thought out. . . . When I have recently written something on a subject, but have then dismissed the matter from my mind, an additional note sometimes occurs to me when I am not thinking about it at all.[76] He also contrasts the communicative possibilities of poetry and philosophy in terms of their respective audience responses:

The *poet* brings before the imagination pictures of life, human characters and situations, all of which he sets in motion and then leaves it to everyone to think in the case of such pictures as much as his mental powers will allow. For this reason, he is able to satisfy men of the most varied capacities, indeed fools and sages simultaneously. The *philosopher*, on the other hand, does not bring life itself in this way, but the completed ideas he has abstracted therefrom, and now requires that his reader will think in precisely the same way and to just the same extent as he does himself; and so his public will be very small. . . . The poet's work demands of the reader nothing more than an entry into the series of writings that entertain or elevate him and the devotion thereto for a few hours. The philosopher's work, on the other hand, tries to revolutionize the reader's whole mode of thought.[77]

The will operates differently on body and mind.[78] In Schopenhauer this insight is combined with the view that, while humans can look at themselves as belonging to either the sensible or intelligible worlds, only in the intelligible can they see themselves as they are (II, 129–130): "The body is given in two entirely different ways to the subject of knowledge, who becomes an individual only through his identity with it. It is given as an idea in intelligent perception, as an object among objects and subject to the laws of objects. And it is also given in quite a different way as that which is immediately known to every one, and is signified by the word *will*." As a consequence of this insight, there are, so to speak, two "stories" that illustrate every action that an individual performs: "one concerning a series of causative mental volitions (the story of his will) and the other concerning the effects of these volitions (the story—or part of the story—of his body)."[79] Schopenhauer defends this view by means of a Plotinian notion that argues that restrictions on what I can learn from sense perceptions do not apply to knowledge about myself, since the human will reveals itself to everyone directly as an aspect of self-consciousness. Elsewhere he notes:

We can reach the thing-in-itself only by our *shifting . . . the standpoint*, that is to say, by starting from what *is represented* instead of, as hitherto, always merely from what *represents*. But for everyone this is possible with one thing only which is also accessible to him from within and is thus given to him in a twofold way. I refer to his own body which stands out in the objective world precisely as representation in space, but which at the same time proclaims itself to his own *self-consciousness* as *will*.[80]

In the mosaic of statements concerning the will made by Schopenhauer, therefore, the intentions of the reader outlined in the preface and the knowledge of the will known to everyone can be seen to be parts of a single, comprehensive *Vorstellung*.

In both cases, what we know of ourselves, we know by means of personal experience. We frequently engage in self-deception: we labor under the illusion that decisions for or against courses of action are freely made in accordance with will, desire, or intention.[81] In preparing the way for what we do, we grant too large a role to imagination, that is, to projected actions that we fancy the result of ethical motivations. The problem with this method is that the will, of whose presence we are conscious, often operates below the level of consciousness, concealing from us our true motivations.[82] Most of us, as we live our everyday lives, are confined to relatively low stages of knowledge. Through the development of an aesthetic consciousness, some of us are capable of transcending this limitation and ascending to a higher plane of understanding.

This upward movement depends on a process of meditative reflection that takes place in the three classical stages, namely attention, withdrawal, and the exploration of inwardness. First Schopenhauer states that "when we undertake anything, we must leave out of consideration everything else and dismiss the matter from our minds, in order to attend to each thing in its own time, to enjoy or to endure it, and be wholly unconcerned about everything else. We must, therefore, have our thoughts in a chest of drawers, so to speak, one of which we open while all the others remain shut."[83] The second stage, the notion of withdrawal, consists in avoiding customary modes of thought and action, and thus detaching ourselves from the slavery of the will. We can then experience the third stage, which consists in a type of inwardness that eventually gives rise to "aesthetic consciousness." In this respect, Schopenhauer, like Coleridge, achieves aestheticism via asceticism.

Conclusion

These lectures have proposed a model for relating ascetic and aesthetic principles in Western reading practices. This model is one in which the ascetic dimension of reading is given greater value than the aesthetic. Yet the methods used to persuade readers to adopt this approach are universally based on aesthetic criteria.

The archetypal statements of the problem are found in Plato's *Republic* and Augustine's *Confessions*. In these works the stated goal of reading is the ethical improvement of the individual. In order to achieve this end the aesthetic element in literary experience is subjected to criticism, in Plato's case through mimesis, in Augustine's through rhetoric. Both reach the same conclusion, which favors morality over pleasure. The debate introduced into the study of literature by these figures reappears in later authors, for example, in Abelard, Dante, Petrarch, and Montaigne. To the limited selection of views presented in these lectures it would be possible to add other contributors without difficulty—for instance Rousseau, George Eliot, and Tolstoy.

The unexpected conclusion is not that Western readers have always read for enjoyment but that, within such enjoyment, they have consistently included an ethical design. It is not the case that early readers were more ethically oriented than later ones, as the decline in religious metaphysics after Newton and Kant might suggest, but that, despite the reduction in interest in this dimension of thinking, they have remained dedicated to the same objectives. All Western reading, it would appear, has an ethical component, and the value placed on this component does not change much over time.

What changes is the way in which the problem is presented. In Plato, the debate takes place in an oral dialogue; in Augustine, in an autobiography, as a response to the reading, memorization, and recitation of epic verse. The issues do not come clearly into focus in antiquity, when reading is a less important vehicle for serious discourse than speaking, declaiming, or performing, but during late antiquity and the Middle Ages, when the use of contemplative practices based on reading becomes widespread in both lay and religious groups. The notion of an "ascetic reader" reaches its high point between the twelfth and fourteenth centuries. But during the lifetime of Petrarch, and within the evolution of his thinking on the subject, this conception is considerably weakened, since he chooses poetry rather than philosophy or theology as his preferred genre for asking ethical questions. The uncertainties associated with ancient and medieval "spiritual exercises" during the Renaissance have their finest expression in Montaigne's *Essais*. It is the reintroduction of Aristotelian notions of *imaginatio*, beginning in the thirteenth century, that provides the foundation for a positive orientation for the ethics of reading, whence the optimism of figures like Gianfrancesco Pico della Mirandola.

The issues are revived and transformed in the nineteenth century, when two of the chief advocates of aesthetic readership are Coleridge in England and Schopenhauer in Germany. Both develop their positions out of interpretations of

Kant on the topics of memory and imagination. Coleridge adopts the metaphysical view proposed by Plato and Augustine, in which the aesthetic dimension of art is viewed within the problem of time and eternity. In Schopenhauer the application of Kantian principles results in a nonmetaphysical viewpoint on the same subjects. In both authors it is within the individual, and the individual alone, that the highest form of aesthetic criteria are realized. This is the basis for Coleridge's notion of the creative imagination and Schopenhauer's theory of genius.

In Coleridge and Schopenhauer, therefore, the ancient position in which the aesthetic is subordinated to the ascetic is reversed, inasmuch as these thinkers advocate aesthetic theories within which the ascetic dimension is accommodated. The manner in which this is done follows traditional stages of meditation involving attention, withdrawal, and higher insight. However, by the end of World War I, "Platonisms" of the type advocated by Coleridge and Schopenhauer are deprived of their logical foundation by analytical approaches to language and the philosophy of mind. In Virginia Woolf's *To the Lighthouse*, in which some of this thinking is reflected, the climax of the first section of the novel consists in a scene that does not demonstrate how reading provides a foundation for intersubjective communication: it illustrates the view that human minds are isolated, independent, and unable to account for the ontological underpinnings on which theories of human communication have so long been based. And yet in *To the Lighthouse* the ascetic impulse is alive and well: the *phantasiae* of Mr. Ramsay, which result from an emotional rereading of a passage from the Waverly Novels, are rejected in favor of Mrs. Ramsay's self-exploration by means of meditation, which is also inspired indirectly by reading.

The continuity in the ascetic dimension of reading through periods of changing intellectual fashions suggests that some rethinking is necessary about what is meant by the term "asceticism" and how its story is to be told. It may be helpful to abandon the use of "secular" and "religious," both of which designate an acknowledged *institutional* boundary among readers but are not always helpful as a way of characterizing the *analytical* differences between literary works, since, as noted in lecture two, both secular and religious writings possess ascetic and aesthetic dimensions. Western literature passes through phases during which the major institutions controlling the output of texts are first secular, then religious, and finally secular again. But the same relationship between ascetic and aesthetic tendencies among writers is found in all phases of Western reading history. What is notable is not that people, then as now, read for pleasure, but that people now, as then, have an ascetic outlook. As noted, it is the persistence of that outlook and its resistance to change that gives continuity to reading theory since ancient times, however much this continuity may have been obscured in the past century by formalistic trends in criticism.

One of the witnesses to changing attitudes toward reading at the beginning of the modern period was Erasmus, who died in 1536. His goal—the adoption of Christian humanism—was unrealized, and perhaps unrealizable, because of Luther and the rise of Protestantism, which offered the masses an accessible type of Christianity through the translation of the Bible and obviated the need to learn classical languages. The program was impractical, because Erasmus, in his fidelity to ancient thinking, incorporated an element that would have worked against the large-scale communication of the Christian truths he had in mind. This was

the elitism of ancient spiritual practices, which never influenced the masses in a secular or religious form. The ancient philosophers who practiced these exercises were few
in number; so were the Jewish and Christian ascetics who
converted to the religious life, entered isolated communities, and followed solitary careers in search of enlightenment. But Erasmus was right on one point. What has made
it possible for the modern age to retain a hold on ascetic
reading, despite the decline in meditative techniques, is the
mass readership of the age of print, which has existed in the
West since the eighteenth century. The mechanization of
culture, long suspected of destroying the spiritual heritage
of the past, has in fact been one of the chief forces that has
sustained it.

Notes

1. The Reader's Dilemma

1. F. M. Cornford, *The Republic of Plato* (Oxford, 1942), 66.

2. *Rep.* 10.601a; trans. Tom Griffith (Cambridge, 2000), 320.

3. W. J. Verdenius, "Plato's Doctrine of Artistic Imitation," in *Plato: A Collection of Critical Essays, II: Ethics, Politics, and Philosophy of Art and Religion*, ed. Gregory Vlastos (Notre Dame, Ind., 1971), 259–273; on the *Rep.*, 267–269.

4. For Augustine's knowledge of the *Rep.*, probably based on Cicero, see *De Civ. Dei* 2.14, where Plato's banishment of the poets from his commonwealth is approved.

5. *Conf.* 1.16.25–26.

6. *Conf.* 1.13.20; trans. Henry Chadwick, *Saint Augustine: Confessions* (Oxford, 1991), 15, somewhat modified.

7. *De Civ. Dei* 1.3; trans. Henry Bettenson (Harmondsworth, 1984), 8.

8. *Poetics* 1449b, 24–28; on the relation to Lessing and other German authors concerned with the imagination, some of whom influenced Coleridge, discussed in chapter 3, see the enduring essay of Jacob Bernays, "Aristotle on the Effect of Tragedy," trans. J. and J. Barnes, in *Articles on Aristotle 4: Psychology and Aesthetics*, ed. Jonathan Barnes, Malcolm Schofield, and Richard Sorabji (London, 1979), 154–165.

9. *Conf.* 3.2.2; trans. Chadwick, pp. 35–36.

10. H.-I. Marrou, *A History of Education in Antiquity*, trans. G. Lamb (New York, 1964), 70–72.

11. Robert A. Kaster, *Guardians of Language: The Grammarian and Society in Late Antiquity* (Berkeley, 1988), 322, points out

that Augustine's teaching methods are not the same as those of his youthful masters. On the later development see Martin Irvine, *The Making of Textual Culture: "Grammatica" and Literary Theory*, 350–1100 (Cambridge, 1994), chaps. 2–3.

12. *Rep.* 3.387b–390a.

13. Thomas A. Szlezák, *Reading Plato*, trans. G. Zanker (London, 1993), 39–46; and in greater depth Franco Trabbatoni, *Scrivere nell'anima: Verità, dialettica e persuasione in Platone* (Florence, 1994).

14. On the prehistory, see Raymond J. Starr, "The Circulation of Literary Texts in the Roman World," *Classical Quarterly* 37 (1987), 213–223.

15. On Jerome's contribution, see Megan Hale Williams, *The Monk and the Book: Jerome and the Making of Christian Scholarship* (Chicago, 2006).

16. On this theme, see Eric A. Havelock, *Preface to Plato* (Cambridge, Mass., 1963).

17. *Conf.* 1.13.20; trans. Chadwick, p. 15.

18. On the notion of a literary *topos*, I follow the guidelines of Ernst Robert Curtius, *European Literature and the Latin Middle Ages*, trans. Willard R. Trask (New York, 1953), chap. 5.

19. On authenticity of the correspondence, see the review of John Marenbon, *The Philosophy of Peter Abelard* (Cambridge, 1997), 82–93; cf. Giles Constable, "Sur l'attribution des *Epistolae duorum amantium*," *Académie des Inscriptions et Belles-Lettres: Comptes rendus des séances de l'année* 2001 *(novembre–décembre)*, Paris, 2001, 1679–1693. Recent scholarship on the correspondence is ably reviewed by Jean-Yves Tilliette, "Introduction," *Lettres d'Abélard et Héloïse*, ed. Éric Hicks and Thérèse Moreau (Paris, 2007), 9–35.

20. Abélard, *Historia Calamitatum*, ed. J. Monfrin (Paris, 1962), 71–75.

21. Betty Radice, trans., *The Letters of Abelard and Heloise* (Harmondsworth, 1974), 66n1.

22. See Nikolaus M. Häring, "Abelard Yesterday and Today," in *Pierre Abélard, Pierre le Vénérable* (Paris, 1975), 343–355; and on the manuscript evidence, 379–381.

23. *Historia*, p. 70, lines 256–258.

24. *Historia*, p. 71, lines 284–286: "Que cum per faciem non esset infima, per habundantiam litterarum erat suprema."
25. *Heloise sue ad ipsum deprecatoria*, ed. Monfrin, *Abélard*, p. 114, lines 127ff.; 115, 186ff.
26. For a recent assessment of these issues, see Guy Lobrichon, *Héloîse: l'amour et le savoir* (Paris, 2005), 15–33.
27. *Historia*, pp. 72–73, lines 332–339: "Quid plura? Primum domo una conjungimur, postmodum animo. Sub occasione itaque discipline, amori penitus vaccabamus, et secretos recessus, quos amor optabat, studium lectionis offerebat. Apertis itaque libris, plura de amore quam de lectione verba se ingerebant, plura erant oscula quam sententie; sepius ad sinus quam ad libros reducebantur manus, crebrius oculos amor in se reflectebat quam lectio in scripturam dirigebat."
28. On this possibility, based on an Avignon manuscript, see Pierre de Nolhac, *Pétrarque et l'humanisme*, vol. 1 (Paris, 1907), 46–47, and Excursus VI, pp. 290–291.
29. *Historia*, p. 73, lines 351–359.
30. If not in a third role, namely as surrogate father, assuming that she was illegitimate; see Enid McLeod, *Héloïse*, 2nd ed. (London, 1971), 11.
31. *Heloyse . . . deprecatoria*, p. 116, lines 231ff.
32. *Conf.* 6.15.25.
33. For a review of the extensive writings in this genre in the twelfth century, see Peter von Moos, *Consolatio: Studien zur mittellateinischen Trostliteratur über den Tod und zum Problem der christlichen Trauer* (Munich, 1971), 199–463.
34. *Heloyse . . . deprecatoria*, p. 116, lines 3–4.
35. Ibid., line 103; cf. 1 Cor. 3:6.
36. Ibid., lines 207ff.
37. Peter the Venerable, *Ep.* 115, ed. Giles Constable, *The Letters of Peter the Venerable* (Cambridge, Mass., 1967), 303–308.
38. For a guide to interpretation over the past two centuries, see Antonio Enzo Quaglio, "Francesca da Rimini," in *Enciclopedia Dantesca*, vol. 3 (Rome, 1971), 1–13, with a bibliographical guide (to 1968), 12–13; for a line by line analysis, see Natalino Sapegno, ed., *La Divina Commedia*, vol. 1 (Florence, 1955), 53–67; for illustrations, see *Dantes göttliche Komödie: Drucke und Illustrationen*

aus sechs Jahrhunderten, ed. Lutz S. Malke (Leipzig, 2000), 83, 147, and 155. For recent studies of canto 5, see the relevant sections of *Studi danteschi* and *Storia della letteratura italiana*, vol. 14, ed. Enrico Malato (Rome, 2004), 115–122.

39. Giovanni Boccaccio, *Il comento alla divina commedia e gli altri scritti intorno a Dante*, vol. 2, ed. Domenico Guerri (Bari, 1910), 137–146.

40. *Inferno*, canto 5, vv. 82–84; trans. John D. Sinclair.

41. *Inferno*, canto 5, vv. 119–120; I am tempted to capitalize *Amore*, which is advisable, I believe, in the circumstances, since *Amor* plays a role comparable to Boethius's *Philosophia* in the *Consolatio Philosophiae*; see the following note.

42. *Inferno*, canto 5, vv. 121–123; Boethius, *Cons. Phil.*, 2, pr. 2, 4.

43. Cf., *Paradiso*, canto 16, vv. 13–15; for a useful discussion, see Renato Poggioli, "Tragedy or Romance? A Reading of the Paolo and Francesca Episode in Dante's *Inferno*," *Publications of the Modern Language Association of America* 72 (1957), 350–351n19.

44. See Adolf Katzenellenbogen, *Allegories of the Virtues and Vices in Medieval Art*, trans. Alan J. P. Crick (London, 1939; repr., Toronto, 1989), s.v. *luxuria*.

45. *Conf.* 13.18; trans. Chadwick, p. 283.

46. In this paragraph I draw on my essay "Reading, Ethics, and the Literary Imagination," *New Literary History* 34.1 (2003), 1–17.

47. *Conf.* 11.26.33; *CCSL*, vol. 27, p. 211, lines 19–21.

48. *Secretum*, lib. 2, ed. Enrico Carrara, in Francesco Petrarca, *Prose*, ed. G. Martellotti et al., 122: "Imo vero inter legendo plurimum; libro autem e manibus elapso assensio simul omnis intercidit."

49. Gur Zak, "Writing from Exile: Petrarch's Humanism and the Ethics of Care of Self," Ph.D. dissertation, Toronto, 2007, chapter one.

50. For an introduction to this theme, see Albert Russell Ascoli, "Access to Authority: Dante in the *Epistle to Cangrande*," in *Seminario Dantesco Internazionale*, vol. 1 (Florence, 1994), 309–310, with a useful bibliography.

51. *De Trin.* 15.13.22.

52. *Rerum Vulgarium Fragmenta*, no. 17, lines 1–8; quoted from Francesco Petrarca, *Canzoniere: "Rerum Vulgarium Fragmenta,"* ed. Rosanna Bettarini, vol. 1 (Turin, 2005), 76; and *Biblioteca Italiana, Canzoniere* (2003), trans. James Wyatt Cook, *Petrarch's Songbook: Rerum Vulgarium Fragmenta, a Verse Translation*, intro. Germaine Warkentin (Binghamton, N.Y., 1996), 41, 43.

53. Quoted from *Astrophel and Stella* in *Sir Philip Sidney: Selected Prose and Poetry*, ed. Robert Kimbrough, 2nd ed. (Madison, 1983), poem 1, lines 1–8.

54. Cf. Marc Fumaroli, *Le genre des genres littéraires français: La conversation* (Oxford, 1992), 4–6.

55. M. A. Screech, "Introduction," in *Michel de Montaigne: The Complete Essays* (London, 1991), xiii.

56. The erudite editor of the *Essays*, Pierre Villey, argued that Augustine's *Confessions* was not a major influence, based on the absence of direct quotations; *Les sources et l'évolution des Essais de Montaigne*, 2nd ed. (Paris, 1933), vol. 2, p. 321; cf. Pierre Courcelle, *Les Confessions de saint Augustin dans la tradition littéraire* (Paris, 1963), 379. However, in contrast to *Contra Academicos* and *De Civitate Dei*, which are quoted directly, there are indirect references; see Gisèle Mathieu-Castellani, "Les *Confessions* de saint Augustin dans les *Essais* de Montaigne," in *Lire les "Essais" de Montaigne: Actes du Colloque de Glasgow, 1997*, ed. Noël Peacock and James J. Supple (Paris, 2001), 211–226.

57. E.g., *Theaetetus* 189e–190a.

58. On the antecedents of this theme, see Pierre Hadot, "Spiritual Exercises," in *Philosophy as a Way of Life*, trans. M. Chase, ed. A. I. Davidson (Oxford, 1995), 101–109.

59. See Fausta Garavini, *Mostri e chimere: Montaigne, il testo, il fantasma* (Bologna, 1991), 219–306; cf. Nicola Panichi, *I vincoli del disinganno: Per una nuova interpretazione di Montaigne* (Florence, 2002), 183–212.

60. The many dimensions of reading in Montaigne cannot be taken up in detail here; for a thorough study, see Terence C. Cave, "Problems of Reading in the Essais," in *Essays in Memory of Richard Sayce*, ed. T. Cave et al. (Oxford, 1982), 133–166; for more recent studies, see Mary B. McKinley, "Lire des *Essais*, 1969–1997: Lectures de la lecture," in *Lires les "Essais" de Montaigne,*

15–26, as well as the contributions on specific issues in that volume.

61. The importance of listening may have been suggested by Plutarch, *De Recte Ratione Audiendi*, which was popular during the Renaissance.

62. On this complex question, see André Tournon, *Montaigne: La glose et l'essai*, 2nd ed. (Paris, 2000).

63. Thomas A. Greene, "Dangerous Parleys—Essais 1.5 and 6," *Yale French Studies* 64 (1983), 16–17.

64. For a brilliant discussion of the ethical context of the *Essais*, see Jean Starobinski, *Montaigne in Motion*, trans. Arthur Goldhammer (Chicago, 1985), 9–34, 67–70, 95–120. For an excellent historical examination, see Hugo Friedrich, *Montaigne*, 2nd ed. (Bern, 1967), chaps. 3–5.

65. René Descartes, *Discours de la Méthode* (1637), *discours* 1.

66. See Richard H. Popkin, *The History of Skepticism from Erasmus to Spinoza*, 2nd ed. (Berkeley, 1979), and Charles B. Schmitt, *Cicero Scepticus: A Study of the Influence of the "Academica" in the Renaissance* (The Hague, 1972).

67. Virginia Woolf, *To the Lighthouse*. Quotations are from the standard text, indicated by section and chapter.

68. William St Clair, *The Reading Nation in the Romantic Period* (Cambridge, 2004), 221.

69. The latter problem was possibly inspired by Woolf's reading of Bertrand Russell's *The Analysis of Mind* (1921); see Gillian Beer, "Hume, Stephen, and Elegy in *To the Lighthouse*," *Essays in Criticism* 34.1 (1984), 33–55; cf. David Daiches, *Virginia Woolf*, revised ed. (New York, 1963), 82.

70. Erich Auerbach, *Mimesis: The Representation of Reality in Western Literature*, trans. Willard R. Trask (Princeton, 1953), 538.

71. E. M. Forster, *Virginia Woolf: The Rede Lecture*, 1941 (Cambridge, 1942), 19.

2. The Ascetic Reader

1. Arthur Schopenhauer, *The World as Will and Idea*, 2nd ed. (1844), trans. R. B. Haldane and J. Kemp (London, 1887), book 4, p. 506.

2. Max Weber, *Wirtschaft und Gesellschaft*, 5th ed., ed. J. Winckelmann (Tübingen, 1972), 542.

3. For a review of the extensive literature on this topic, see Johannes Winckelmann, ed., *Max Weber: Die protestantische Ethik II; Kritiken und Anti-kritiken*, 2nd ed. (Hamburg, 1972); more broadly, Wolfgang Schluchter, *The Rise of Western Rationalism: Max Weber's Developmental History*, intro. G. Roth (Berkeley, 1981).

4. Otto Zöckler, "Asceticism, (Christian)," in *Encyclopedia of Religion and Ethics*, ed. James Hastings, vol. 2 (New York, 1909), 74; cf. Zöckler, *Kritische Geschichte des Askese: Ein Beitrag zur Geschichte christlicher Sitte und Kultur* (Frankfurt, 1863); *Askese und Monchtum* (Frankfurt, 1897).

5. On Pythagoras and Pythagorean traditions, see N. W. De Witt, "Organization and Procedure in Epicurean Groups," *Classical Philology* 31 (1936), 205–211; on Plato, see *Rep.* 7.536d–e, and the discussion in Pierre Hadot, *What Is Ancient Philosophy?* trans. Michael Chase (Cambridge, Mass., 2002), chap. 5.

6. *De Ordine* 2.8.25 and 2.20.53.

7. See Guy G. Stroumsa, "Un nouveau souci de soi," in *La fin du sacrifice: Les mutations religieuses de l'Antiquité tardive* (Paris, 2005), 23–60.

8. See the comprehensive study of this theme in Peter Brown, *The Body and Society: Men, Women, and Sexual Renunciation in Early Christianity* (New York, 1988).

9. *Collationes*, ed. E. Pichery, 3 vols (Paris, 1955–1959), vol. 1, I, II, p. 79.

10. Ibid., vol. 1, I, XVIII, pp. 98–100.

11. Ibid., vol. 1, VII, IIII, p. 248.

12. Ibid., vol. 1, VII, VI, pp. 251–253.

13. See Gaston Hocquard, "Solitudo Cellae," in *Mélanges Louis Halphen* (Paris, 1951), 323–234.

14. *Collationes*, vol. 1, VII, XXI, pp. 262–265.

15. Ibid., vol. 1, VII, p. 84.

16. Ibid., vol. 2, IX, II, pp. 40–41.

17. Ibid., vol. 2, XII, III, pp. 124–125.

18. Ibid., vol. 2, IX, XXV–XXVI, pp. 61–62.

19. Ibid., vol. 1, III, VI, pp. 145–146.

20. *Quod Omnis Probus Liber Sit*, cc. 80–82.

21. *De Vita Contemplativa*, cc. 24–29; later, a similarly Stoic view is found in 4 Maccabees.

22. Palladius, *Historia Lausiaca* 3.15.

23. *Historia Monachorum*, 31.

24. Ibid., 42.

25. Athanasius, *Vita Antonii*, trans. Evagrius, cc. 72–77.

26. *Life of Abbi, Patrologia Orientalis*, vol. 17, p. 215. For an equally vivid account of the tears accompanying holy reading and meditation, see Besa, *The Life of Shenoute*, cc. 94–95, trans. David N. Bell (Kalamazoo, 1983), 70.

27. Gunnar Olinger, ed., *A Letter of Philoxenus of Mabbug Sent to a Friend* (Acta Universitatis Gotoburgensis 56, 1950), 16–17.

28. In this section I draw on my essay "Ethics and the Humanities: Some Lessons of Historical Experience," *New Literary History* 36 (2005), 7–12, as subsequently.

29. The classic introduction to *lectio divina* remains Jean Leclercq, *The Love of Learning and the Desire for God: A Study of Monastic Culture*, trans. Catherine Misrahi (New York, 1961); a useful review of the main tendencies is found in the collective article "Lectio divina et lecture spirituelle," in *Dictionnaire de Spiritualité*, vol. 9 (1976), 470–510.

30. Isidore of Seville, *Sententiae*, lib. 3, c. 8.3 and 8.6; PL 83.679B, 680A.

31. Ibid., 3, 9.4; PL 83.681A: ". . . de otio spirituali."

32. Joseph de Ghellinck, "'Pagina' et 'Sacra Pagina': Histoire d'un mot et transformation de l'objet primitivement désigné," in *Mélanges Auguste Pelzer* (Louvain, 1947), 23–59.

33. Hugh of St. Victor, *De Scripturis et Scriptoribus Sacris*, c. 1; PL 175.10D.

34. Pseudo-Augustine, *Sermo* 219, *In Vigiliis Paschae*; PL 38.1088. The idea was reiterated by later authors, e.g., Alcuin, *De Virtutibus et Vitiis*, c. 5; PL 101.616D; *Ep.*, 51, PL 100.216C.

35. Smaragdus, *Diadema Monachorum*, c. 3, *De lectione*; PL 102.507C.

36. See P. Aubin, "Intériorité et extériorité dans les *Moralia in Job* de saint Grégoire le Grand," *Recherche de sciences religieuses* 62 (1974), 117–166. Cf. Carol Straw, *Gregory the Great: Perfection in Imperfection* (Berkeley, 1988).

37. *In. Ep. Ad Galat., quaest.*, 19; PL 175.560B–C: "Nota tria

esse silentia. Primum silentium est ignorantia languoris, quod fuit sub lege naturali. Secundum silentium est desperatio salutis, quod fuit sub scripta lege. . . . Tertium silentium est adeptio sanitatis: quod erit in gloria aeternae beatitudinis." 38. On modes of silence in Greek patristic and medieval texts, see I. Hausherr, "L'Hesychasme," *Orientalia Christiana periodica* 22 (1956), 5–40, 241–285.

39. For an introduction to this aspect of monastic literary tradition, see Jean Leclercq, "Culte liturgique et prière intime dans le monachisme au moyen âge," in *Aux sources de la spiritualité occidentale* (Paris, 1964), 285–303.

40. For an excellent review of the relevant themes see the lecture of Hagen Keller, "Vom 'heiligen Buch' zur 'Buchführung': Lebensfunktionen der Schrift im Mittelalter," *Frühmittelalterliche Studien* 26 (1992), 1–31; on the sociological implications, see Alois Hahn, "Zur Soziologie der Beichte und anderer Formen institutionalisierter Bekenntnisse: Selbstthematisierung und Zivilisationsprozess," *Kölner Zeitschrift für Soziologie und Socialpsychologie* 3 (1982), 408–434. A brief authoritative review of the principles of meditation is found in the article "Méditation" by Emmanuel von Severus and Aimé Solignac, in *Dictionnaire de Spiritualité*, vol. 10, cols. 906–914.

41. See Aviad M. Kleinberg, *Prophets in Their Own Country: Living Saints and the Making of Sainthood in the Later Middle Ages* (Chicago, 1992); *Histoire des saints: Leur rôle dans la formation de l'Occident* (Paris, 2005).

42. See Paul Saenger, "The British Isles and the Origin of the Modern Mode of Biblical Citation," *Syntagma: Revista del Instituto de Historia del Libro y de la Lectura* 1 (2005), 77–123.

43. See Corrado Bologna, "L'invenzione' dell'interiorità (spazio della parola, spazio del silenzio: monachesimo, cavalleria, poesia cortese)," in *Luogi sacri e spazi della santità*, ed. Sofia Boesch Gajano and Jucetta Scaraffia (Turin, 1990), 243–266.

44. Etienne Gilson, "Guigue I le Chartreux: Méditations," *La Vie Spirituelle* 40 (1934), 165.

45. Cf. Leclercq, *The Love of Learning*, 23–24.

46. For further discussion, see my essay "Lectio Spiritualis," in *After Augustine* (Philadelphia, 2001), 101–114.

47. For the relevant statements on this theme between Gregory

the Great and Jean Gerson, see Louis Gougaud, "Muta Praedica-tio," *Revue bénédictine* 42 (1930), 168–171; a useful synthesis with an excellent bibliography is Lawrence G. Duggan, "Was art really the 'book of the illiterate'?" *Word and Image* 5 (1989), 227–251. On the Byzantine tradition, see Gilbert Dagron, *Décrire et peindre. Essai sur le portrait iconique* (Paris, 2007).

48. Among the numerous studies of these issues see Suzanne Lewis, "The English Gothic illuminated Apocalypse, *lectio divina*, and the art of memory," *Word and Image* 7 (1991), 1–32; on later medieval techniques, see Sixten Ringbom, "Devotional Images and Images of Devotion," *Gazette des Beaux-Arts* 73 (1969), 159–170; Jeffrey F. Hamburger, "Speculations on Speculation: Vision and Perception in the Theory and Practice of Mystical Devotion," in *Deutsche Mystik im abendländischen Zusammenhang*, ed. Walter Haug and Wolfram Schneider-Lastin (Tübingen, 2000), 353–408; for an excellent study of a single manuscript and its illustrations, see Niklaus Largier, "Der Körper der Schrift: Bild und Text am Beispiel einer Seuse-Handschrift des 15. Jahrhunderts," in *Mittelalter: Neue Wege durch einen alten Kontinent* (Stuttgart, 1999), 241–271; on illustrations of the oral mode, see Jesse M. Gellrich, "The Art of the Tongue: Illuminating Speech and Writing in Later Medieval Manuscripts," in *Virtue and Vice: The Personifications in the Index of Christian Art*, ed. Colum Hourihane (Princeton, 2000), 93–119.

49. See the extensive study of meditative techniques on this theme in Fritz Oskar Schuppisser, "Schauen mit den Augen des Herzens: Zur Methodik der spätmittelalterlichen Passionsmeditation, besonders in der Devotio Moderna und bei den Augustinern," in *Die Passion Christi in Literatur und Kunst des Spätmittelalters*, ed. Walter Haug and Burghart Wachinger (Tübingen, 1993), 169–210.

50. David M. Lindberg, "Alhazen's Theory of Vision and Its Reception in the West," *Isis* 58 (1962), 321–341.

51. Leclercq, *The Love of Learning*, 155. The connection seems normal by the time of William of Malmesbury (d. c. 1143), who refers to it by means of neologism; *Gesta Regum Anglorum*, ed. R. A. B. Mynors, R. M. Thomson, and M. Winterbottom (Oxford, 1998), vol. 1, p. 150: "Diu est quod et parentum cura et meapte dili-

genta libris insuei. . . . Hinc est quod, ab antiquo scriptus non contentus, ipse quoque *scripturire* incepi." (My italics.)

52. See the extensive review of the issues in Nikolaus Staubach, "Pragmatische Schriftlichkeit im Bereich de Devotio moderna," *Frühmttelalterliche Studien* 25 (1991), 418–461.

53. See Paul Saenger, *Space Between Words: The Origins of Silent Reading* (Stanford, 1997); cf. Armando Petrucci, *Scrivere e leggere nell'Italia medievale* (Milan, 2007), 43–63, 99–124, and 153–164.

54. See the excellent study of Sarah Spence, *Texts and the Self in the Twelfth Century* (Cambridge, 1996).

55. *Liber de Modo Bene Vivendi ad Sororem, Praefatio,* PL 184.1199B.

56. Philip of Harvengt, *De Silentio Clericorum,* c. 6, PL 203.849C–850B.

57. Adam of Dryburgh, *Liber de Ordine, Habitu, et Professione Canonicorum, Sermo* 9.12; PL 198.530A.

58. Ibid., *Sermo* 12.15; 577B.

59. Ibid.

60. Ibid., 14.11; 601D.

61. Garnier of Rochefort, Sermo 2, PL 205.573D–574A.

62. Ibid., 593B, 594A.

63. Summarizing *De Peccato Originali,* liber 2, PL 160.1081B.

64. The influential eighteenth-century study of this theme, which drew on ancient and medieval material, is J. G. Zimmerman, *Solitude,* Eng. trans. (London, 1798).

65. *Utopia,* in *The Complete Works of St. Thomas More,* vol. 4, ed. Edward Surtz, S.J., and J. H. Hexter (New Haven, 1965), 1; echoed by Gerhard Geldenhauer, ibid., 30. In the epigraph a possible *double entendre* arises out of the use of *libellus,* which can mean a "little book" or a "satirical work," as in Suetonius, *Julius Caesar,* 80, etc.

66. Guillielmus Budaeus Thomae Lupseto . . . , in *Complete Works,* 9–10. The association dates from the patristic period; cf. Augustine, *De Ordine* 2.20.53.

67. See Arthur O. Lovejoy's suggestive if uncompleted essay, "The Communism of St. Ambrose," in *Essays in the History of Ideas* (New York, 1960), 296–307.

68. Guillielmus Budaeus . . . , in *Complete Works*, p. 7. The theme is taken up by Raphael Hythlodaeus in book 2, ibid., vol. 4, p. 165.

69. Ibid., 13.

70. Ibid., pp. 49, 51, and 180.

71. Ibid., 56.

72. Ibid., 103; cf. 105.

73. Ibid., 103.

74. Ibid., 105.

75. *Republic* 5.416d.

76. *Complete Works*, vol. 4, pp. 123 and 126.

77. Ibid.; cf. 158.

78. Ibid., 128; cf. Plato, *Laws* 1.643b–c, 7.797a–b.

79. J. H. Hexter, "Introduction," in *Complete Works*, vol. 4, p. lxxiv.

80. Ibid., ciii (I have capitalized *Askese*).

81. *Complete Works*, vol. 4, p. 158.

82. Ibid., 160.

83. Ibid., 160, 162; my trans.

84. Ibid., 160, 166.

85. See Lorenzo Valla, *De Voluptate*, published in 1431; see D. C. Allen, "The Rehabilitation of Epicurus and His Theory of Pleasure in the Early Renaissance," *Studies in Philology* 41 (1944), 1–15; Jill Kroge, "Moral Philosophy," in *The Cambridge History of Renaissance Philosophy*, ed. Charles B. Schmitt (Cambridge, 1988), 374–386.

86. *Complete Works*, vol. 4, in order pp. 166, 226, and 228.

87. Ibid., 166, 168, 170.

88. *De Finibus*, I.x.33, I.x.36.

89. *Complete Works*, vol. 4, p. 162.

90. Ibid.: "Rationem porro, mortales primum omnium in amorem, ac uenerationem diuinae maiestatis incendere . . ."; my trans.

91. Ibid.; my trans.

92. Ibid., 162, 166.

93. Ibid., 174, 176, 178.

94. Ibid., 178; trans. modified.

95. Ibid., 219.

96. See Louis Martz, *The Poetry of Meditation* (New Haven,

1954). I draw here on my paper "La lecture d'Augustin et la littérature anglaise au XVIIe siècle," *sous presse.*

97. Quoted from *The Poems of George Herbert*, intro. Helen Gardner, 2nd ed. (London, 1961), 31.

98. Descartes, *Meditatio* 2; Augustine, *Sol.* 2.7: [Aug.] "Deum et animam scire cupio."

99. *Oxford Latin Dictionary* (Oxford, 1976), s.v.

100. Leclercq, *The Love of Learning*, 24–25.

101. Descartes, *Meditationes de Prima Philosophia*, ed. Geneviève Rodis-Lewis (Paris, 1978), 8–9.

102. *Meditatio* 1, p. 19: "Opportune igitur hodie mentem curis omnibus exsolvi, securum mihi otium procuravi, solus secedo, serio tandem et libere generali huic mearum opinionum eversioni vacabo."

103. *Discours de la méthode*, ed. E. Gilson, 5th ed. (Paris, 1976), 4.

3. The Aesthetic Reader

1. Quoted in the Loeb Classical Library, trans. H. Rushton Fairclough (Cambridge, Mass., 1978), 478–479.

2. Ibid.; my trans.

3. Hugh of St. Victor, *De Scripturis et Scriptoribus Sacris*, c. 1, PL 175.10D–11D.

4. *Inferno*, canto 4, v. 94.

5. Sir Philip Sidney, *The Defence of Poesy*, c. 3, "Propositio," Kimbrough, ed., *Sir Philip Sidney: Selected Prose and Poetry*, 109–110. On Plato, as enemy, see c. VI, "Refutatio," p. 141, and, for Plato's alleged repudiation of this view, pp. 142–143.

6. See Florence Dupont, "*Recitatio* and the reorganization of the space of public discourse," in *The Roman Cultural Revolution*, ed. Thomas Habinek and Alessandro Schiesaro (Cambridge, 1997), 44–59.

7. On the Renaissance restatement of this belief, see Sydney, *Defence of Poesy*, c. II, "Narratio," in *Selected Prose*, 103–109.

8. On Plato's indirect acknowledgment of this point with respect to Homer, see *Ion* 537a–539d.

9. For an excellent review of the word's history, see "Phanta-

sia," *Historische Wörterbuch der Philosophie*, vol. 7 (Basel, 1989), cols. 515–535; on early developments, see Gerard Watson, "The Concept of 'Phantasia' from the Late Hellenistic Period to Early Neoplatonism," in *Aufstieg und Niedergang der römischen Welt*, Bd. 36.7 (Berlin, 1994), 4765–4810.

10. *Oxford English Dictionary*, q.v.

11. Gerard Watson, *Phantasia in Classical Thought* (Galway, 1988), 60.

12. Which does not, of course, always involve the use of poetic imagery.

13. An early study is Murray Wright Bundy, *The Theory of Imagination in Classical and Mediaeval Thought* (University of Illinois Studies in Language and Literature, 12.2–3, Urbana, Ill., 1927), 19–59; for a more recent view, see Gerard Watson, *Phantasia in Classical Thought*, 1–13; cf. Watson, "Discovering the Imagination: Platonists and Stoics on *phantasia*," in *The Question of "Eclecticism": Studies in Later Greek Philosophy*, ed. John M. Dillon and A. A. Long (Berkeley, 1988), 208–233.

14. *Sophist* 184d; Watson, *Phantasia*, p. 4.

15. *Theaetetus* 189e–190a; Watson, *Phantasia*, p. 5.

16. Cf. *Sophist* 263e; *Philebus* 38c–e; Augustine, *Soliloquia* 2.7.13–14.

17. *Phaedrus* 275ab, 275de, trans. Alexander Nehamas and Alexander Woodruff, in Plato, *Complete Works*, ed. John M. Cooper and D. S. Hutchinson (Cambridge, 1997).

18. *Philebus* 39a–b, trans. Dorothea Frede, in Plato, *Complete Works*. Augustine utilizes *phantasia* to explain Dan. 5:5, where Balthazar sees the fingers of a hand writing on a wall; *De Genesi ad Litteram* 12.11.23.

19. Thomas McFarland, *Coleridge and the Pantheist Tradition* (Oxford, 1969), 113, quoting in order *Notebooks*, ed. K Coburn (New York, 1957 ff.), vol. 1, p. 1064; *S. D. Coleridge's Treatise on Method . . .* , ed. Alice D. Snyder (London, 1934), 38; and *The Friend*, Essay VII, in Samuel Taylor Coleridge, *Collected Works*, vol. 2, p. 429. Cf. McFarland, *Coleridge and the Pantheist Tradition*, pp. 34–35, who traces this view to Shaftesbury and to Plato, not, in the latter case, with success.

20. For a more detailed survey, see Watson, *Phantasia in Classical Thought*, chaps. 2–4.

21. E.g., *Metaphysics* 991a.

22. Cf. Bundy, *The Theory of Imagination*, 67.

23. Cicero, *Acad.* 1.4.13–18, from which Augustine derives his view; cf. Sextus Empiricus, *Adv. Math.* 7.227; Diogenes Laertius, *Vitae* 7.46; cf. 7.54.

24. Diog. Laer. 7.46.

25. Watson, *Phantasia in Classical Thought*, 56.

26. See Édouard Jeauneau, *Quatre thèmes érigéniens* (Montreal, 1978), 34–46.

27. On the literary consequences of this rhetorical notion of *mimesis*, see the enduring study of Erich Auerbach, *Mimesis*; originally published as *Mimesis: dargestellte Wirklichkeit in der abendländischen Literatur* (Bern, 1946).

28. See Deborah L. Black, *Logic and Aristotle's 'Rhetoric' and 'Poetics' in Medieval Arabic Philosophy* (Leiden, 1990), chaps. 3 and 7.

29. *Ep.* 7.2.4. Augustine's original terms for the divisions were (1) *sensis rebus inpressum*, (2) *putatis*, and (3) *ratis*. However, by the time he wrote *De Musica*, book 6, he was familiar with the terms *phantasia* and *phantasma*, which he used thereafter. For an application, see *De Trin.* 8.5.8, where the distinction is made between the memory of justice, permanently lodged in the mind, and impermanent *phantasiae* and *phantasmata*.

30. The distinction is reused by the anthropologist Frederick C. Bartlett as the basis for discussing social memory: *Remembering: A Study in Experimental and Social Psychology* (Cambridge, 1932).

31. *Conf.* 10.8.14.

32. *De Civ. Dei* 11.18.

33. *De Libero Arbitrio*, book 1.

34. *De Civ. Dei* 11.1.

35. *Vita Nuova*, c. 1.

36. Ibid., 2.1; cf. *Purg.*, canto 17, vv. 13ff.

37. The text is taken from *Canzoniere . . .* , ed. Rosanna Bettarini (2005), 13, and the *Biblioteca Italiana*; the translation is by Robert Durling, *Petrarch's Lyric Poems: The 'Rime sparse' and Other Lyrics* (Cambridge, Mass., 1976), 38.

38. See Martin Kemp, "From 'Mimesis' to 'Fantasia': the Quattrocento Vocabulary of Creation, Inspiration and Genius in the Visual Arts," *Viator* 8 (1977), 347–398.

39. He was the author of a life of his uncle, Giovanni Pico della Mirandola, which was translated by Thomas More. *Utopia* provides an illustration of the positive uses for the imagination described in *De Imaginatione*, although there is no evidence that More was acquainted with the work. The harm done to politics by unbridled fantasies (cc. 6–7) is emphasized in book 1 of *Utopia*.

40. Gianfrancsco Pico della Mirandola, *On the Imagination*, ed. and trans. Harry Caplan (New Haven, 1930), c. 5: ". . . omnem sensualis animae interiorem vim. . . ." Trans. modified.

41. Ibid., c. 6; trans. slightly modified.

42. Ibid., c. 7. Cf. c. 10, where Christ is described as overcoming sense and imagination by reason and intellect (p. 70).

43. See Arthur O. Lovejoy, "Coleridge and Kant's Two Worlds," in *Essays in the History of Ideas*, 254–276.

44. *Biographia Literaria or Biographical Sketches of My Literary Life and Opinions*, ed. James Engell and W. Jackson Bate, in Coleridge, *Collected Works*, vol. 7, pp. 304–305.

45. For a negative assessment of Coleridge's originality on this question, see the classic statement of René Wellek, *History of Modern Criticism, 1750–1950* (New Haven, 1955), vol. 2, pp. 151–153, and for an influential response, McFarland, *Coleridge and the Pantheist Tradition*, 14–52. On the distinction in English writers see John Bullitt and W. J. Bate, "Distinctions between Fancy and Imagination," *Modern Language Notes* 60 (1945), 8–15.

46. For Kant, see *Kritik der praktischen Vernunft*, ed. Benzoin Kellermann, in *Immanuel Kants Werke*, in Gemeinschaft mit Hermann Cohen *et al.*, ed. Ernst Cassirer (Berlin, 1912–1922), vol. 5, section 49, p. 389.

47. *The Prelude* (1805), ed. E. de Selincourt, rev. H. Darbyshire (Oxford, 1959), book 12, lines 376–377.

48. *Biographia Literaria*, chap. 10, in *Collected Works*, vol. 7, p. 168.

49. Although not, oddly, Plato's *Timaeus*, which would have supported his views; he claims not to have understood it.

50. E. R. Dodds, "Tradition and Personal Achievement in the Philosophy of Plotinus," in *The Ancient Concept of Progress and other Essays on Greek Literature and Belief* (Oxford, 1973), 136.

51. McFarland, *Originality and Imagination* (Baltimore, 1985), 91–93, 102–104.

52. Quoted and translated by McFarland, ibid., 103.

53. *Biographia Literaria*, lxxxvi.

54. Ibid., lxxxviii, xxx.

55. On the resulting principles of criticism and their evolution, see J. R. de J. Jackson, *Method and Imagination in Coleridge's Criticism* (London, 1969), 48–74; on links with German critical thought, see E. S. Shaffer, "The Hermeneutic Community: Coleridge and Schleiermacher," in *The Coleridge Connection: Essays for Thomas McFarland*, ed. Richard Gravil and Molly Lefebure (London, 1990), 200–229.

56. For an account of meditation in Coleridge, see Reeve Parker, *Coleridge's Meditative Art* (Ithaca, 1975), 63–89.

57. *Philosophical Lectures*; quoted in McFarland, *Pantheist Tradition*, 207n2.

58. Ibid., 186; McFarland, ibid., 208n5.

59. *Biographia Literaria*, xc, xcii.

60. Ibid., xciv; see the well-documented account in McFarland, *Coleridge and the Pantheist Tradition*, 112–116.

61. *Biographia Literaria*, lxxxvi.

62. *The Mirror and the Lamp: Romantic Theory and Critical Tradition* (New York, 1953), 346n57; for Lovejoy, see "Coleridge and Kant's Two Worlds," 254–276.

63. McFarland, *Coleridge and the Pantheist Tradition*, 23.

64. It is possible that Plotinus was absorbed through Schelling, who was indebted to his thinking; see Fritz Heinemann, *Plotin: Forschungen über die plotinische Frage, Plotins Entwicklung, und sein System* (Leipzig, 1921), 318; more generally, see P. F. Reiff, "Plotin und die deutsche Romantik," *Euphorion* 19 (1912), 591–612. However, Coleridge read Plotinus himself, and may have found in Schelling confirmation for an already established direction for his thinking. In this respect, Schelling may have stimulated Coleridge toward metaphysical speculation in the way that Plotinus stimulated the young Augustine.

65. Arthur Schopenhauer, *The World as Will and Idea*, 2nd ed. (1844), trans. R. B. Haldane and J. Kemp (London, 1883), 22. Quotations from *Die Welt as Wille und Vorstellung* from this translation

are indicated by book and page number within the text. On the importance of dreams in Schopenhauer, see the extensive discussion in his "Essay on Spirit Seeing and everything connected therewith," in *Parerga and Parilipomena*, trans. E. F. J. Payne, 2 vols (Oxford, 1974), vol. 1, pp. 227–309.

66. Among the assumptions that he rejects are those of Fichte, Schleiermacher, and Hegel; see "Sketch of a History of Ideal and Real: Appendix," in *Parerga and Paralipomena*, vol. 1, pp. 23–24; cf. Patrick Gardiner, *Schopenhauer* (Harmondsworth, 1967), 13–14.

67. "Fragments for the History of Philosophy," in *Parerga and Paralipomena*, vol. 1, p. 100.

68. "Ideas concerning the Intellect," in *Parerga and Paralipomena*, vol. 2, pp. 41–42.

69. "Counsels and Maxims," in *Parerga and Paralipomena*, vol. 1, pp. 433–434; cf. 440–441.

70. On the debt to Plato, see "Fragments for the History of Philosophy," 43–46, where it is noteworthy that Schopenhauer relies on Sextus Empiricus (*Adv. Math.* 7.116 and 119) for a summary of Platonic doctrines. Despite his pessimism on other subjects, Schopenhauer does not echo Plato's negative attitude toward the pleasure derived from some aesthetic experiences. Nor does he include Augustine among the philosophers, despite his mention of more obscure figures, such as Johannes Scottus Eriugena, who derived many ideas from the bishop of Hippo; cf. "Transcendent Speculation on the Apparent Deliberateness in the Fate of the Individual," in *Parerga and Paralipomena*, vol. 1, p. 219, where two notions on predestination are discussed.

71. Cf. Augustine, *De Doctrina Christiana*, book 1, chap. 4.

72. Gardiner, *Schopenhauer*, 28, quoting Schopenhauer's doctoral dissertation, *"On the Fourfold Root of the Principle of Sufficient Reason,"* section 34.

73. "On Philosophy and its Method," in *Parerga and Paralipomena*, vol. 2, p. 9. Note, however, that Augustine is not one of the forerunners of this view listed by Schopenhauer, which includes pagan and Christian Neoplatonism, Gnosticism, and the thought Johannes Scottus Eriugena; ibid., 10. Augustine's paternity of the Western version of this distinction is widely acknowledged.

74. Schopenhauer's connections with Eastern religious thought

are scrutinized by Moire Nicholls, "The Influences of Eastern Thought on Schopenhauer's Doctrine of the Thing-in-Itself," in *The Cambridge Companion to Schopenhauer*, ed. Christopher Janaway (Cambridge, 1999), 171–212.

75. "On Philosophy at the Universities," in *Parerga and Paralipomena*, vol. 1, p. 160. See pp. 160–164 for a strong criticism of the abuse of writing and publishing in post-Kantian philosophy. On the role of reflective activity in artistic production, see "Counsels and Maxims," 438–441.

76. "Ideas Concerning the Intellect," 55–56; cf. *The World as Will and Idea*, 2.14.

77. "On Philosophy and its Method," 3, in *Parerga and Paralipomena*, vol. 2, pp. 4–6.

78. Augustine, *Confessions* 8.9.21. Although Seneca, Augustine, and Luther may be the most important formative influences on Schopenhauer's conception of the will, he expresses his admiration for the writings on the subject by Johannes Scottus Eriugena: "Fragments for the History of Philosophy," 61–64.

79. Gardiner, *Schopenhauer*, 157.

80. "Fragments for the History of Philosophy," 93; Schopenhauer's emphasis.

81. This thinking is not indebted directly to Augustine but accords well with the views expressed in book 1 of *De Libero Arbitrio*.

82. "Fragments for the History of Philosophy," 162–163, 174–176.

83. "Cousels and Maxims," 437.

Index

Abba Or, 56
Abbi, 57
Abelard, Peter, 7–13, 18, 19, 20,
    22–24, 26, 41, 42, 47, 66–67,
    135
Abrams, M. H., 120
Adam of Dryburgh, 72
Addison, Joseph, 119
Aeneas, 2, 59, 77
Akenside, Mark,119
Alan of Lille, 77, 112
Alcuin, 148n34
Allen, D. C., 152n85
Ambrose, St., 54, 62, 75
Ammonius Saccas, 52
Amor, 17, 18, 19, 20–21, 25, 109,
    110, 144n41
Anselm of Canterbury, St., 71, 88
Antony, St., 56, 89–90, 91
Aquinas, Thomas, St., 71, 81
Aristobulus of Paneas, 52
Aristophanes, 84
Aristotle, 3, 35, 84, 94, 98, 101–
    102, 104, 112, 113
Arthur, King, 21
Ascoli, Albert Russell, 144n50
Athanasius, St., 54
Aubin, P., 148n36
Auerbach, Erich, 146n70, 155n27
Augustine of Hippo, St., 1–7,
    9, 13, 20, 21, 22–25, 26, 27,
    28, 29, 30, 31, 32, 33, 35–36,
    46, 47, 49, 51, 54, 58–59, 61,
    62, 66, 71, 73, 74, 75, 81, 84–
    92, 96, 98, 99, 103–107, 108,
    111, 112, 122, 125–126, 135,
    141–142n11, 145n56, 151n67,
    155n23, 155n29, 157n64,
    158n70, 158n71, 159n78,
    159n81
Augustinus (in *Secretum*), 26–
    31, 88

Balthazar (Dan. 5:5), 154n18
Bankes, William, 41
Barnes, Jonathan, 141n8
Barthes, Roland, 5
Bartlett, Frederick C., 155n30
Bate, Walter Jackson, 156n44,
    156n45
Beer, Gillian, 146n69
Bell, David N., 148n26
Bembo, Pietro, 33–34
Benedict of Nursia, St., 59–60,
    68, 90
Berkeley, George, 119
Bernard Silvestris, 77, 112
Bernard of Clairvaux, St., 63, 71–
    72, 90
Bernays, Jacob, 141n8
Bettarini, Rosanna, 33, 145n52,
    155n37

Index

Index

Index

Hobbes, Thomas, 116
Hocquard, Gaston, 147n13
Homer, 1, 2, 4, 59, 84, 96
Horace, (Quintus Horatius Flaccus), 28, 30, 93–97
Hourihane, Colum, 150n48
Hugh of St. Victor, 60, 62, 65, 94
Hume, David, 116, 129
Hutchinson, D.S., 154n17
Hythlodaeus, Raphael, 76–78

Ignatius of Loyola, St., 70, 85–86, 89–90
Irvine, Martin, 142n11
Isidore of Seville, St., 60
Islam, 69
Isocrates, 96

Jackson, J. R. de J., 157n55
Jainism, 48, 51
Janaway, Christopher, 159n74
Jean de Meun, 112
Jeauneau, Édouard, 155n26
Jerome, St., 6, 12, 95
Jesuits, Order of, 89
John of Damascus, St., 69
Johnson, Samuel, 97, 116–117
Josephus, Flavius, 55–56
Judaism, 52–53, 56, 64, 69, 80, 82, 95, 139
Julian of Norwich, 68, 86
Justin Martyr, St., 52

Kant, Emmanuel, 114–115, 116–117, 118–119, 212, 122, 129, 136–137
Kaster, Robert, 141–142n11
Katzenellenbogen, Adolf, 144n44
Keller, Hagen, 149n40
Kellermann, Benzoin, 156n46
Kemp, J., 157–158n65
Kemp, Martin, 155n38
Kempe, Marjorie, 86
Kimbrough, Robert, 145n53, 153n5

Kleinberg, Aviad M., 149n41
Kroge, Jill, 152n85

Lancelot du Lac, 21–22, 24–25
Largier, Niklaus, 150n48
Laura, (in Petrarch's poems), 87–88, 109–111
Leclercq, Jean, 148n29, 149n39, 149n45, 150n51, 153n100
Lefebure, Molly, 157n55
Leibniz, Gottfried Wihelm, 115, 118
Lessing, Gotthold Ephraim, 141n8
Lewis, Suzanne, 150n48
Lindberg, David M., 150n50
Lobrichon, Guy, 143n26
Locke, John, 116, 119
Long, A. A., 154n13
Longinus, Cassius, 98, 103
Lovejoy, Arthur O., 151n67, 156n43, 157n62
Luther, Martin, 49, 159n78

Malatesta da Riminio, 14
Malato, Enrico, 144n38
Malke, Lutz S., 144n38
Manichaeism, 51
Marcus Aurelius, 64–65
Marenbon, John, 142n19
Marrou, H.-I., 141n10
Martellotti, G., 144n48
Martin, St., 53
Martz, Louis, 152n96
Marvell, Andrew, 86
Mathieu-Castellani, Gisèle, 145n56
McFarland, Thomas, 120–121, 154n19, 157n51, 157n52, 157n57, 157n58, 157n60, 157n63
McKinley, Mary B., 145–146n60
McLeod, Enid, 143n30
Metellus of Tegernsee, 94

164

Index

Milton, John, 96
Misrahi, Catherine, 148n29
Monfrin, Jacques, 142n20,
    143n25
Monica, St., 62
Montaigne, Michel de, 26, 35–39,
    47, 129–130, 135, 136
Montanism, 52
Moore, G. E., 42
More, Thomas, St., 52, 75–85,
    156n39
Moreau, Thérèse, 142n19
Mt. Ventoux, ascent of, 27
Mynors, R. A. B., 150n51

Nahamas, Alexander, 154n17
Neoplatonism, 34, 51–52, 53, 59,
    68, 81, 89, 98, 105, 117, 158n73
Newton, Isaac, 136
Nicholls, Moire, 158–159n74
Nietzsche, Friedrich, 65

Odo of Cambrai, 73
Olinger, Gunnar, 14827
Origen, 52

Pachomius, St., 53
Palladius, 53–54, 56
Panichi, Nicola, 145n59
Paolo Malatesta, 13–25
Paraclete, convent of the, 9, 10
Parker, Reeve, 157n56
Pascal, Blaise, 65
Paul, St., 9, 52–53, 75, 143n35,
    148–149n37
Payne, E. F. J., 158n65
Peacock, Noël, 145n56
Pelagianism, 81
Peter the Venerable, 13
Petrarch, Francesco, 8, 26–38, 47,
    86–88, 94, 104–105, 108, 109–
    111, 112, 123–124, 135
Petrarchism, 33–35

Petrucci, Armando, 151n53
Philip of Harvengt, 72
Philo of Alexandria, 52, 55–56
Philostratus, 98
Philoxenus of Mabbug, 56
Pichery, E., 147n9
Pico della Mirandola, Gianfran-
    cesco, 113–114, 136
Pico della Mirandola, Giovanni,
    156n39
Pindar, 122
Plato, 1–7, 13, 22, 24, 29, 33, 35,
    36, 47, 51, 52, 59, 75, 76, 78,
    84, 95–96, 97, 98–102, 104,
    105, 106–108, 111, 112–113,
    115, 119–119, 120–122, 125–
    126, 128, 135, 136, 141n4,
    147n5, 153n5, 154n19, 156n49,
    158n70
Pliny the Younger, 55–56, 97
Plotinus, 32, 111, 117, 121, 132,
    157n64
Plutarch, 35, 98, 146n61
Poggioli, Renato, 144n43
Popkin, Richard H., 146n66
Porphyry, 51
Portinari, Beatrice, 108–109, 111
Pythagoras, 51, 75

Quaglio, Antonio Enzo, 143n38
Quintilian (Marcus Fabius Quin-
    tilianus) 58, 98
Quirinus, St., 94

Radice, Betty, 142n21
Ramsay, James, 45
Ramsay, Mr., 39–46, 137
Ramsay, Mrs., 39–46
Ravenna, 14–15
Reiff, P. F., 157n64
Richardson, Samuel, 11
Ringbom, Sixten, 150n48
Rousseau, Jean-Jacques, 15, 135
Russell, Bertrand, 42

Index

Saenger, Paul, 149n42, 151b53
Sapegno, Natalino, 144n38
Scaraffia, Jucetta, 149n43
Schelling, Friedrich Wilhelm
  Josoph von,116–117, 121,
  157n64
Schiesaro, Alessandro, 153n6
Schlegel, August Wilhelm von,
  101
Schlegel, Friedrich von, 101
Schleiermacher, Friedrich Daniel
  Ernst, 158n66
Schluchter, Wolfgang, 147n3
Schmitt, Charles B., 146n66,
  152n85
Schneider-Lastin, Wolfram,
  150n48
Schofield, Malcolm, 141n8
Schopenhauer, Arthur, 48, 114,
  115, 122–134, 136–137
Schuppisser, Fritz Oskar, 150n49
Scott, Walter, 40–41, 43, 137
Screech, Michael, 35
Seneca, 11, 28, 51, 58, 60, 66, 77,
  82, 96, 98, 159n78
Sextus Empiricus, 103, 155n23,
  158n70
Shaffer, E. S., 157n55
Shaftesbury, Anthon Ashley
  Cooper, 154n19
Shakespeare, William, 101,
  122–125
Sidney, Sir Philip, 34, 94, 113
Sinclair, John D., 144n40
Skepticism, 38–39
Slezák, Thomas A., 142n13
Smaragdus of St. Mihiel, 61
Snyder, Alice D., 154n19
Socrates, 1, 4, 36, 96, 99, 100, 105
Solignac, Aimé, 149n40
Sophocles, 84, 122
Sorabji, Richard, 141n8
Spence, Sarah, 151n54

Spinoza, Benedict, 120
St Clair, William, 146n68
St. John of the Cross, St., 85
Starobinski, Jean, 146n64
Starr, Raymond J., 142n14
Staubach, Nikolaus, 151n52
Stoicism, 11, 38, 51, 68, 82–83,
  102–103, 104, 105
Straw, Carol, 148n36
Strousma, Guy G., 147n7
Suetonius Tranquillus, Gaius,
  151n63
Supple, James J., 145n56
Surtz, Edward, S.J., 151n63
Symenon of Studion, 62

Tacitus, Cornelius, 97
Tansley, Charles, 40–41
Taylor, Thomas, 117
Tertullian, Quintus Septimius,
  52
Tetens, Johann Nicolaus,
  118–119
Theodoret, bishop of Cyrrhus,
  53–54
Therapeutae, 55–56
Theresa of Ávila, St., 85
Thomas à Kempis, St., 70
Thomas of Celano, St., 63
Thomson, R. M., 150n51
Thucydides, 84
Tilliette, Jean-Yves, 142n19
Tolstoy, Leo, 135
Tournon, André, 146n62
Trabbatoni, Franco, 142n13
Traherne, Thomas, 86
Troeltsch, Ernst, 49

Ulysses, 76, 77
Utopia, 75–85

Valla, Lorenzo, 96
Vaughan, Henry, 86

166

Index

Verdenius, W. J., 141n3
Vergil (Publius Vergilius Maro),
   2, 3, 4, 15, 16–17, 19, 22, 28,
   31, 59, 96, 120
Vespucci, Amerigo, 77
Villey, Pierre, 145n56
Vlastos, Gregory, 141n3
von Moos, Peter, 143n33
von Severus, Emmanuel, 149n40

Wachinger, Burghart, 150n49
Warkentin, Germaine, 145n52
Watson, Gerard, 102,
   153–154n9,154n13
Weber, Max, 49–51, 80, 89–90
Wellek, René, 156n45

William of Malmesbury, 150n51
Williams, Megan Hale, 142n15
Winckelmann, Johannes, 147n3
Winterbottom, M., 150n51
Witt, N. W., 147n5
Wittgenstein, Ludwig, 42
Wolff, Christian, 119
Woodruff, Alexander, 154n17
Woolf, Virginia, 7, 39–46, 47, 137
Wordsworth, William, 111, 117,
   119
Wyatt, Thomas, 34

Zak, Gur, 29
Zimmermann, J.G., 15n64
Zöckler, Otto, 147n4